Joel

Shirley Hamilton

Contents:

Preface

This book seemed an obvious Old Testament choice after the study on the book of Revelation from the end of the New Testament. The word of God stands complete and consistent with itself and therefore the two books were going to be complimentary to each other.

The people of Joel's day faced a great judgement of God, such that we also face in these end times of human history. The message and the situation is so relevant to us and cogent with the cultural times we live in. I wanted to sound the call for us to look again at the message of the prophet Joel and see it is for us in our day and learn spiritual lessons from it.

This is a devotional commentary and I hope it will be a help and encouragement to you as you face these difficult days in which we live.

I owe gratitude to the work of John Gill, John Calvin and Matthew Henry specifically for guiding me in the interpretations of my mind and also many faithful teachers of the Word of God over the years of my Christian life. I am deeply thankful to God for the work of the Holy Spirit in my life and in my mind that He has given me, and that God has enabled me to think and write in this way.

I pray for blessing on all who read this book and that you will now the power of God as you seek Him and His truth.

Introduction:

Joel was a prophet of the Lord, approximately 800BC, but it is very unclear exactly when he lived and worked for the Lord his God. His name means "The Lord is God" and his proclamation speaks the Word of the Lord to his generation and all after him, according as he is included in the Holy Scriptures. Joel may have been a contemporary of the prophet Isaiah and after the prophets Amos and Micah.

The book cites calamity, especially in the first chapter, which strikes the farming community with great destruction and desolation.

"Hear this, you elders, And listen, all you inhabitants of the land. Has this ever happened in your days, or in the days of your fathers?"

Joel 1:2

This is a calamity of calamities and brings total desolation to the land of Judah and death and disease to the people. It is a pestilence from the Lord and the land is brought to economic and social ruin by it. The whole countryside is destroyed and those who tend the fields and vineyards are reduced to poverty and sorrow. There is an outpouring of the grief in chapter one, and this is developed through the three chapters of the book to show the spiritual desolation of the people of God and the restoration by the power of the Spirit of God.

There are no sacrifices to the Lord in this calamity because there is no provision for the people. The prophet calls for restoration and that the people repent and return to the Lord their God.

"Mourn like a virgin dressed in sackcloth for the husband of her youth."

Joel 1:8

The return to God must be sincere and sacrificial and the Lord will relent and heal their land.

The prophet Joel also points us to the situation in these last days, when God's Spirit will be poured out on all His people and there will be an ingathering of people from every kindred, tribe and tongue.

These last days have cataclysmic calamity waiting to happen to our earth, and the people of God are kept safe from this. It is a time of great conflict and trouble.

"I will show wonders in the heavens and on the earth, blood and fire and pillars of smoke. The sun will be turned to darkness and the moon to blood before the coming of the great and awesome Day of the LORD."

Joel 2:30-31

This apocalyptic writing denotes what is coming in future days and could be happening right now in our world. The Lord is not slack concerning His promises and He has promised to deliver His holy people, and so he will.

"And in that day the mountains will drip with sweet wine, and the hills will flow with milk. All the streams of Judah will run with water, and a spring will flow from the house of the LORD..."

Joel 3:18

Whatever happens around us, the Lord will not forsake those who love Him. The future is bright even though all around seems dark and foreboding. The prophet Joel reminds us of the mercy of the Lord when all around gives way to conflict, loss and destruction. Those who put their trust in Him are never confounded.

Joel Chapter One

20 verses

Joel Chapter One

V1 Joel

"The Word of the Lord that came to Joel, the son of Pethuel."

This book of the prophet Joel is the Word of the Lord to us in our day, and in all days of history. Because it is the Word of God, we need to pay careful heed to it, to meditate and learn what it says and put its teaching into the practice of our life. The Word of God never changes in any generation and this word is as cogent to us now as it was to the people all those millennia ago. The circumstances might change but the principles and direction of the Lord does not.

Joel is chosen to relay this message to us, as a set-apart and devoted servant of the Lord. The prophets suffered much as a result of their message, for it was not popular and they and their message were rejected by their own people. The words of Joel are authenticated in the New Testament by the Apostles Peter and Paul and quoted in Acts chapter two. His words refer to that coming time when the Spirit of God would be poured out and all people would be blessed by the message of the gospel.

Joel is the son of Pethuel. When the Scripture expresses family ties in this way, it is indicating a godly father and family situation. It is thought that Pethuel was the son of the prophet Samuel, but I am unclear about this. If it is so, then the family line is intact by the mercy of God and through the faithful lives of Hannah, Samuel and Pethuel and now, Joel.

God does not necessarily save families. God saves all those who come to Him in repentance and faith, and He deals with the individual and has individual relationships with His people. We do not have "Christian families" "Christian countries" and the like. We must all stand as individual beings before the holy God to give account of what we have done in the body. When The prophet Joel calls for repentance, it means that every soul must come to God and seek Him and seek forgiveness, not as a body of amorphous people, but as repentant sinners before God. God sees us all and we must close with Him in a personal way. He seeks those who will repent and believe and will give their will and heart to Him.

"Tear your heart, and not your garments, and turn to the Lord, your God; for he is gracious and merciful, slow to anger, and abundant in loving kindness, and relents from sending calamity."

Joel 2:13

This is not a national symbolic act but the exercise of true contrition to God for our personal sin and seeking forgiveness and a new start. This is the key message from the Lord in the book of Joel. When the people repent and turn, then the healing of the nation can begin. God is full of compassion for us in our weakness and destitution and will heal both us and our land when we repent. Joel is the faithful messenger of this message from God.

V2 Listen

"Hear this, you elders, And listen, all you inhabitants of the land. Has this ever happened in your days, or in the days of your fathers?"

There is great responsibility in being an elder or a leader in a situation. We are all accountable to God, but those who have been given authority are more strictly measured and more closely accountable. It is a heavy duty to take upon oneself, in becoming a director of people and not a situation to gain importance or personal kudos for oneself. Joel calls the leaders to hear what he has to say, and not be proud in their attitude towards the Word of the Lord.

"Let not many of you be teachers, my brothers, knowing that we will receive heavier judgment."

James 3:1

However, we are all accountable to God for our life and conduct. The prophet is addressing everyone, all the inhabitants of the land, and is charging them to listen and pay close attention to what he says. We also are constrained to listen to our God and to pay close attention to His commands and requirements. He is the LORD...

A dreadful physical calamity has occurred in the land, and locusts have destroyed everything. They have stripped the crops and neither the humans nor the animals have anything to eat. People are dying and the whole economic and social structure of the country has broken down and lawlessness is setting in.

Joel asks the rhetorical question....

Nothing like his has ever happened before in the history of the nation and the people along with the elders are devastated as the land has been stripped bare. This devastation is so intense and complete that no one can remember such a thing happened before. God has sent a severe trial to the people that no one in preceding generations has experienced.

Joel is speaking up about it and calls the people and their leaders to listen to him and hear what he has to say, for it is a

message from the Lord to help them
through warning.

V3 Tell

"Tell your children about it, and have your children tell their children, and their children, another generation."

To rehearse the truths of God and all He has done for us is such a spread of the blessing. We are to tell the generations what the Lord has done and teach them the character of God as we discuss life. The purposes and acts of God should be part of our speaking and we should not be embarrassed to discuss with others what the Lord has done for us.

Why do we not do this naturally? Are we ashamed of our Lord?

This catastrophic event that has happened to the people of God, has stopped them in their tracks and God is going to show them a demonstration of His delivering power and teach them wonderful things about Himself that they can pass on to the succeeding generations in their families and nation. The glory of the Lord will be seen and experienced, and a warning will also be included. To rehearse our failures and demonstrate the forgiveness and

mercy of the Lord is so wonderful. This is
the witness of the Christian life and the
humble way that we share the truth of
God.

Perhaps we are unwilling to admit our
failures or to praise the name of the Lord
for all He has done for us. Perhaps we
ourselves fail to rehearse the deliverance
of the Lord and therefore forget what we
have been saved from. Perhaps we are
insensible to His ways of working and
don't even notice what He is doing in our
lives.

*"I will remember the deeds of the Lord;
for I will remember your wonders of old. I
will also meditate on all your work, and
consider your doings. Your way, God, is in
the sanctuary. What god is great like
God?"*

Psalm 77:11-13

 We remember by the constant rehearsing
of the blessings of the Lord and specifically
the glory of salvation. We need to meet at
the table of remembrance and break the
bread and drink the wine that
commemorates the death of the Lord
Jesus for us. We must not neglect the

daily study of the Word of God, for we forget so easily and quickly. Prayer should be our daily breath as we live in the presence of the Lord and in the consciousness of the Holy Spirit.

"Call to me, and I will answer you, and will show you great things, and difficult, which you don't know."

Jeremiah 33:3

V4 Locust

"What the swarming locust has left, the great locust has eaten. What the great locust has left, the grasshopper has eaten. What the grasshopper has left, the caterpillar has eaten."

This catastrophic event that Joel cites for us here, takes the form of a massive and uncountable number of destroying locusts that have come upon the land and stripped it bare. The Lord has been thorough. Each succeeding wave of attack strips away what the last one overlooked. There are so many – billions of them, they cannot be counted. They are merciless and ruthless as they strip the earth of all growing things and leave barrenness and destitution behind them. Nothing stops them. Locusts are notorious for destroying all plants and green life in the environment. They are relentless and did great damage to the Egyptians at the time of the Exodus. Here they are again but in greater numbers. They are sent by the Lord to do His work in the lives of His people.

We say, "it is too much Lord... why?"

This is the constant and universal cry of God's people when trouble arises, and we are sorely oppressed. We see the hand of God as being against us, and we complain and think that it is unjust treatment from the Lord. Our cry is "it's not fair!" God does not deal with His people in judgment but in mercy. If we received justice, we would be in utter darkness and punishment forever. God is merciful and deals with us as He sees fit, and that is right for us. Those who are trusting in Him will see that and remain faithful, whereas the impenitent will blame the Lord and fall away. Only when we remember that all that is sent to us, is sent in mercy, do we bring our troubles to Him, examine ourselves and seek the Lord.

When we are young in the faith, we all go through this thought process and have to learn our lesson from the Lord. No matter how oppressive the trial is, He gives us the strength to face it and will shoulder even blame, so that we can sort out our thinking and our crisis of faith.

There are many reasons why God sends trouble. This huge oppression was to test the people of God and to warn them against turning away from God. It was a precursor to worse judgment should they not return to their God. It was to bring home to them the reality of the coming Day of the Lord and imprint on their mind the holiness of the Lord in His intolerance of evil.

Beloved, let us listen to the voice of the Lord, so that trouble will not come and may we learn from the Word of the Lord, rather than receive chastisement and pains. God loves His people and will not permit us to be taken away by temptation, sin and this world, but will train us to trust and obey Him and serve Him only.

If you are not yet found by Christ, you must seek the Lord, for the Day of the Lord will surely come and you must be ready to meet Him.

V5 Weep

"Wake up, you drunkards, and weep! Wail, all you drinkers of wine, because of the sweet wine; for it is cut off from your mouth."

God gives us all things richly to enjoy. We take His blessings and enjoy them, but we can find ourselves using and abusing them for the feeding of our own desires. Things that are a blessing can become a curse to us. Alcohol is mentioned here as something that people do to excess and indulge themselves in its pleasures. The people have become so indulgent that they are called "drunkards" by the Lord, for they have replaced the love of God for the love of substances. This could be applied to almost anything. Some indulge in food, shopping, inappropriate romances, family bonds, internet games, films, violence... almost anything can take that treasured place close to our Almighty God. We can find ourselves valuing anything more than Him and not to delight to draw near to him in personal fellowship.

The people of God in this time of Joel are indulging themselves in ungodly living and enjoying themselves to the detriment of their devotion and service to God. God calls out to them about their preoccupations and shouts at them to waken up. He has now suddenly taken away the thing that is fascinating them and is putting them in very uncomfortable circumstances. All the streams of their pleasures have now dried up and they are left in the cold light of day. God tells them to weep. They are to come to their senses and realise what has happened to them and seek the Lord. Their pleasures are gone, and their temptations are evaporated, and they now face the cold reality of their situation before God.

We can find ourselves in this dilemma quite easily, when we stop examining our hearts and motives every day and stop keeping short accounts with God. We easily slide into indulgent behaviours and soon find that the pleasures of this life take over from our delight in God. We stop thinking about Him, or don't have the time to spend with Him and become hardened to the delights of His presence, becoming happy with the good things of this life and spiritual exercise and activities become tedious to us. Before long we fall away and become lackadaisical about our spiritual life and we find ourselves attracted to the things we need to avoid. Often, we fall into some sin, as a temptation comes along and we easily succumb, for it seems attractive to us. Our defences are down, for we have laid off our spiritual life with God and the world and our sinful self takes over.

It can happen so quickly and so effortlessly, for it is our natural inclination. The fires of our spiritual life need the daily attention and fellowship with the Lord our God, if we are to be over-comers.

The people of God have found themselves in this state and are now suffering the discipline of their Lord, as he seeks to divert them from worse consequences of their sinful mindset and life-style. They have avoided the weeping for their sin, and now they have it in a great amount. Weeping over our weaknesses and failures is a healthy place to be, and we can bring them to the Lord for He will abundantly pardon us and give us the strength to be victorious. God will bring His people into a good place again, but for the moment, it is time to face up and take account of what is happening.

V6 Teeth

"For a nation has come up on my land, strong, and without number. His teeth are the teeth of a lion, and he has the fangs of a lioness."

This text likens the swarm of locusts that have come against the people of God, as being like an invading army. So they are, and they have decimated everything. They might be seemingly small in themselves but the sheer number of them have overwhelmed the land and left the people destitute. It seems the hand of the Lord is against His people. It seems like punishment, and we automatically begin to think it is more than is deserved.

We can feel like this in our Christian life, as the circumstances and experiences of our life seem to overwhelm us and cause us so much sorrow. We think the mercy of the Lord has left us and we have missed the mark so badly, that God has given up on us. We think we cannot cope and heap up worry and negativity to ourselves and start distrusting God or thinking that He is not in control. Some days are just difficult, and the enemy comes in like a flood, like a swarm of sharp-toothed invaders! We may not be able to work out exactly why, and at times our comfort seems far away, but we know and remember the Lord is near. No matter how troublesome is the trouble He will provide a way of escape and pour in the oil and the wine.

There are times that can be devastatingly difficult. These locust invaders are described as lions and lionesses, with sharp teeth and able to tear us apart. We are not spared such distresses, but the Lord is able to succour us and help us to face the foe and look to Him in our times of trial. He will not let His people be torn apart by the troubles of life and will supply all our need according to His mercy and resources in the Spirit. We take our refuge in His word and remember His sure and precious promises and are sustained. The fangs and teeth may be bared against the people of God, but His protecting love is ever with them.

These unrelenting swarms of locusts have come against the people, and the people are suffering, but God's purposes are to purify His people and not to harm them. Whatever we are facing, God knows what we can bear and has a long-term purpose of blessing on us. God will not allow the enemy to destroy us but will protect and save His people from the teeth of the enemy.

Beloved, let us trust in Him and persevere under the trials and find the victory in our redeemer and Saviour, Jesus.

V7 Stripped

"He has laid my vine waste, and stripped my fig tree. He has stripped its bark, and thrown it away. Its branches are made white."

The Lord likens His people to a vine. Jesus also refers to us as the branches of the vine, as he is the true vine. Those who trust in Him are branches attached to the true vine and are alive and safe in His sustaining care. The people of God in Joel's day had gone away from the Lord and were suffering under the chastising hand of the Lord. The Lord says that these oppressors of His people have cause them a lot of trouble and have laid them waste and stripped them bare. It is a picture that reminds us of the work of the locusts who have destroyed the land and now the effects of this are destroying the spiritual fabric in the lives of the people who are suffering. They are like branches that have been stripped of all foliage and are suffering the ravages of troubles.

Often the physical suffering that we experience has an effect on our spiritual lives for good or for ill. We either react in faith or in resentment. Those who are familiar with the love of God will know His comfort and strength and will see the value of the troubles and be able to be thankful for them. However, at this time, the vine of life is laid waste and the fig tree is stripped of its luscious foliage and fruit. The bark of the covering of life is striped way and the bare flesh is revealed. The branches have become unprofitable and there is need of deep renewal and a fresh lease of life for them. The people of God are decimated because of their disobedience and lack of spiritual regard, and God has laid them bare to the ravages of the army of the locusts. They are truly destroyed by famine and war and are unprofitable servants.

Still, there is hope, for the Lord will not lift His hand against His people forever. He is able to restore them and show love and life to them. Even the most terrible devastation to the land by the locusts can be renewed. The Lord will again restore them, through their repentance and a turning back to Him. When we suffer the pains of our sin and folly, even as Christian believers, we will be renewed in Christ, and He will enable us to stand up under the trouble. We must seek the Lord and examine our thought patterns and behaviour that we will be renewed and bear fruit again for Him.

"No temptation has taken you except what is common to man. God is faithful, who will not allow you to be tempted above what you are able, but will with the temptation also make the way of escape, that you may be able to endure it."

1 Corinthians 10:13

God will again renew His vine and the fig tree will again bear fruit and flourish. Let us not be unprofitable and ruin our life with God by staying away from Him. Let us learn our lessons and have the faith to move on with the Lord, in the full armour of salvation.

"Therefore put on the whole armour of God, that you may be able to withstand in the evil day, and having done all, to stand."

Ephesians 6:13

V8 Mourn

"Mourn like a virgin dressed in sackcloth for the husband of her youth!"

The saddest of situations is when the one you loved is gone or has left you. The Lord requires the same deep heartfelt mourning for sin and the steadfast desire to turn away from it. God likens it to the sadness we feel when our nearest and dearest are gone, and we are left alone. The heart wrenching sadness and sorrow of loss is so great and causes us such deep distress. The sense of rejection and isolation can be almost impossible to cope with, except for the strength of the Lord. In our distresses we seek the Lord and find our peace and comfort in Him. We must embrace the Word of God, hold on to it and find help in the things around us that he has given us to do.

This deep sorrow is the same sorrow we should be feeling about our sins and weaknesses. Only when we feel the sorrow will we turn away, for often our hearts are hard and we ignore the warnings of Scripture. We serve a mighty God who is patient with us and willing to forgive us repeatedly, but we seek holiness and therefore the avoidance of sins will be our number one concern. There are times we feel sorry for our sin, but do we actually mourn over it? Do we feel pain that we disappoint the Lord and other people?

We can easily hide from our own hearts and imagine we are good enough. There are always sins to fight and to be put away from us.

"The Lord is not slow concerning his promise, as some count slowness; but he is patient with us, not wishing that anyone should perish, but that all should come to repentance."

2 Peter 3:9

One of God's attributes is His long-suffering nature and His willingness to forgive. He does not punish us as we deserve but is willing to wait for us to come to repentance and bow our will to His holy will. He does not punish His people but will allow them to suffer if it will bring them into a good place and help them to live more godly lives. The Lord wants more of us, not less, and knows that closeness to him is the greatest comfort we possess. Let us cling to Him and find Him to be our all in all.

V9 Offering

"The meal offering and the drink offering are cut off from the Lord's house. The priests, the Lord's ministers, mourn."

The servants of the Lord also are in mourning, because the people are unable to make the usual offerings to the Lord. The Lord has set requirements for the giving of sacrifices and offerings to Him, and for the work of his house. The blessing of the priests and the people are dependent on these offerings, but the catastrophe has stopped the flow of the blessing into the Lord's house. This has a knock-on effect for the servants of the Lord, as they are dependent on the support of the congregation.

God has also set requirements for us about His church, and we are to support our local congregation and the work of the Lord in our area. This is the responsibility of the people of God, and all are included in this. We are to give sacrificially to God and not to be stinting or keep too much for ourselves. God speaks to us about this and promises blessing if we obey him and give to Him.

The offerings that are not being given are the food and drink offerings, which suggests that the close fellowship with the Lord is broken, and these fellowship offerings cannot and are not being offered. This is why they are mourning with the people.

The work of God suffers in our day, because the offerings are small and there are less Christians to support the word of God. We should respond to the needs around us and support our local church with all our efforts. It is important that the work of God will continue, and the servants of God are provided for. This teaching speaks to me and the need to sort out finances so that we can give generously and with an open heart.

It also reminds us that our sin separates us from the Lord, and when we fail and fall we break the fellowship with Him. We must repent and mend our relationship with the Lord who is ever ready to forgive us and restore us.

V10 Waste

"The field is laid waste. The land mourns, for the grain is destroyed, The new wine has dried up, and the oil languishes."

Even the inanimate ground is mourning for the loss of its covering. The fields are now barren because the crops are destroyed, and the vineyards have been stripped bare. There is no grain for the bread, no oil or wine to make the heart glad. The prophet is reiterating what he has said before. The analogy is of the forgotten and diminishing church and work of God. There is no food of the Word to nourish the souls of the people and no oil and wine of gladness and praise for the blessing of God.

The people are sinning and not even noticing but living their lives for themselves. Consequently, they do not repent or return to the Lord, and therefore there is no comfort either.

If we keep short accounts with the Lord, we will not falter but will come to a place of peace and blessing. When trouble and heartache come into our personal life we will have the oil and wine of the comfort of

God to save ourselves from much grief.
Pains do come to us for all kinds of
reasons, but those who are faithful will be
kept by the Lord and comforted.

*"But the Counsellor, the Holy Spirit, whom
the Father will send in my name, will teach
you all things, and will remind you of all
that I said to you. Peace I leave with you.
My peace I give to you; not as the world
gives, I give to you. Don't let your heart
be troubled, neither let it be fearful.*

John 14:26-27

V11 Confounded

"Be confounded, you farmers! Wail, you vineyard keepers; for the wheat and for the barley; for the harvest of the field has perished."

Maybe we are tired of the mourning and the wailing! But this is stronger language. The prophet tells the farmers and the vineyard keepers, that they are accursed. They wail because the hand of the Lord is against them, and they can't help themselves or sort out their own problems. When they think on their situation all their plans are thwarted.

They long for the food and nourishment of the wheat and the barley but the harvest has gone and the crops in all the fields have perished.

In our day, there are many Christian believers who long for the strong meat of the Word of God but cannot find it. The teaching is so shallow and perfunctory that it is hardly worth listening to. There is so much falsehood mixed up with the Scripture that the people are led astray, and the land is in spiritual famine.

The preaching of the life-saving gospel is almost non-existent and there is an emptiness of true conversion experiences where people are turning to the Lord in the repentance of broken-heartedness. There is no change of heart because it is all about being friendly with God and no real understanding of who He is and what He requires from us. Sin is not talked about, and we avoid the feeling of guilt, in case people are "put off." The cycle of liberal belief is then perpetuated and there is a kind of religion born of easy-to-believe Jesus who will help us no matter what we are like. There is no holiness of life preached and so we are not holy.

The people wail for the Word of the Lord, but it has gone.

Beloved, we must call out to the Lord of the harvest that He will again come down and visit His people with truth and the vigour of faith that leads to the reinstating of the gospel and the light will again arise and the crop of the church will again grow.

V12 Withered

"The vine has dried up, and the fig tree withered; the pomegranate tree, the palm tree also, and the apple tree, even all of the trees of the field are withered; for joy has withered away from the sons of men."

The withering of the trees of the gardens and wood are a sign and an analogy for the withering of the spiritual life of the people.

The vine symbolises fruitfulness which has disappeared from the land, leaving barrenness. There is no fruit to God, no offerings or tithes in the storehouse. The fig tree is a sign of prosperity and security. Both these blessing have gone and there is no provision for the people, and they are spiritually destitute. We look into our lives to see the blessing of God and to know we are walking with Him. It is not about our feelings of our thought patterns, but about the faith that clings to Him and the joy that will see us through to the very end. We look into our souls and the outward life of deeds and seek righteousness. The pomegranate tree was a symbol of righteousness, and we must exhibit this grace and gift in our life. We know there is no human righteousness, but if we belong to God, we have the righteousness of Christ to cover us and make us truly right before the holy God. The pomegranate tree has withered, and righteousness is not found among the people of God.

Victory has gone. The things of this earthly life have overtaken the people of God and they are succumbing to temptation and experiencing failure. The withered palm tree speaks of this truth that the prophet is showing the people. The people have lost their personal knowledge of God and the picture of the apple tree speaks of this.

If fact, all the trees are withered and dry. So also, the joy of the people of God has withered, and they can only redeem that joy through repentance and a change in life. We also must not depend on feelings and the provision of life, but on the salvation of the Lord. We put our trust in Him and lay all our burdens at His feet. We do not allow ourselves to let the burdens and stresses of life take away our joy in the Lord but look for His blessing and peace. This is true of those who do not know the Lord. Their fruitfulness is withered, and their life is just dry. Until we seek the Lord, we can never find the rest we crave. Only in Christ is there life and peace with God.

V13 Withheld

"Put on sackcloth and mourn, you priests! Wail, you ministers of the altar. Come, lie all night in sackcloth, you ministers of my God, for the meal offering and the drink offering are withheld from your God's house."

The main burden of the mourning seems to fall on the shoulders of the minsters of the people. The prophet teachs them to put on sackcloth, the symbol of deep mourning in death, because the souls of the people are dying. These ministers and priests are to mourn and wail all night in their sackcloth clothes, so that the burden of the people never leaves them.

The people are reduced to live in their sins and the meal and drink offerings are never presented to the work of God. The offerings are actually withheld deliberately. People know what they are doing and are purposefully neglecting the things of God. The work of God languishes undone, and no one is challenged about their lifestyle choices. The ministers have ceased from their work of tending the flock of God and now they have all gone astray.

The responsibility seems to be laid at the door of the minsters of the Lord. They are singled out for specific and deeply expressive mourning, and they are responsible for letting the people know how deeply God is offended by their recalcitrant behaviour. The priests and ministers model the contrition God requires and the deep humility and pensive repentance that He wants to see in his people.

The offerings will never return unless there is repentance again. This is true in our era of history too. How will our country be saved if we do not repent to the Lord our Maker and turn away from our sin? We go on and on and get worse and worse. Sin is our undoing and so the whole land suffers.

"I will sprinkle clean water on you, and you shall be clean: from all your filthiness, and from all your idols, will I cleanse you. I will also give you a new heart, and I will put a new spirit within you; and I will take away the stony heart out of your flesh, and I will give you a heart of flesh. I will put my Spirit within you, and cause you to walk in my statutes, and you shall keep my ordinances, and do them. You shall

dwell in the land that I gave to your fathers; and you shall be my people, and I will be your God. I will save you from all your uncleanness: and I will call for the grain, and will multiply it, and lay no famine on you."

Ezekiel 36:25-29

The Lord is willing to forgive the humble and repentant heart that turns from its sinful ways and seeks the path of holiness. The only way to repent is before the cross of Christ. Only as we see the man dying on the cruel cross for our sin and feel the full weight of our guilt, will we be made willing to bow our knee and come to Him. Only as we humble our sinful heart and mind, do we find full and free forgiveness and the joy of eternal life in our soul.

Minsters of the gospel carry a heavy burden for the people they serve, and therefore we should be paying for them and upholding them before the Lord. They have grave responsibility and need the constant care of their Saviour and the filling of the Holy Spirit to do their task for the Lord with a true heart and a clear mind.

V14 Sanctify

"Sanctify a fast. Call a solemn assembly. Gather the elders, and all the inhabitants of the land, to the house of the Lord, your God, and cry to the Lord."

In this verse the prophet gives us the remedy for the trouble in the land. He tells the elders to set apart time and space to hold a fast. It is to be a solemn assembly and there will be tears and regret. To be sorry for our sin we have to feel it, repent and experience the delivering power of God. When we cry to the Lord, He hears us.

All the leaders, the elders and the people were in this together. It is important that we become part of a group of God's people so that they can help us and hold us accountable for what we do and how we speak. We can find ourselves running away and not really facing our misdeeds and failures and therefore not really growing in the Christian life. It is crucial to have discipled inner lives because we easily fall into bad habits and start to take short cuts and become lazy. When we are tired our thought processes can become oppressive to us and drag is down. It is crucial that we rehearse the truths of God and not depend on our feelings.

It is really important to meet with the people of God, to worship with them and be taught and encouraged from the Word of God.

We are close to the Lord in His house and it is good to meet there. Solomon was given the task of building the temple and he did it with such care and love that it was an amazing place to be, where the glory of the Lord was celebrated and the beautiful of the decoration reflected the beauty of the Lord.

As we go to the house of God, let us get ourselves ready to worship and learn and rejoice with the sisters and brothers in Christ. Let us reflect openly the goodness of the Lord and His great love for us. We sanctify ourselves to Him and walk worthy of the Lord.

V15 Destruction

"Alas for the day! For the day of the Lord is at hand, and it will come as destruction from the Almighty."

Here we have the first reference to the day of the Lord. This is a huge day of reckoning for the people of God in this time of the Prophet and he is sent that they will face their sins and repent and change their ways. The day of the Lord is in this time, is the visitation of the swarms of locusts that are infiltrating the land and destroying the life of the people and the whole nation. They have brought destruction and death to the land and the people are in mourning along with their priests and leaders.

The day of the Lord is to be feared. This day of the Lord is a precursor and an emblem of days that are to come, namely the complete destruction of Jerusalem in the future when even the temple will be destroyed.

It is also a preview of the Last great day of the Lord, when the whole earth will pass away in fervent heat and all human history will be over. We will all give account for the deeds done in the body and every idle word we have spoken. It will be the last great battle, the battle of Armageddon, when the enemies of the Lord will gather to vent out their fury on the Lord, but to no avail. He will destroy them with a word from His mouth and not a blow will be struck.

In the succeeding verses and chapters, this day will be referred to again and again and is a motif of the future in the book of Joel.

"I will gather all nations, and will bring them down into the valley of Jehoshaphat; and I will execute judgment on them there for my people, and for my heritage, Israel, whom they have scattered among the nations. They have divided my land.."

Joel 3:2

The day of the Lord is surely coming and we must be ready.

The cry goes out in our day... *"the day of the Lord is at hand..."* we must work while it is still day and bring many into the kingdom.

V16 Cut off

"Isn't the food cut off before our eyes; joy and gladness from the house of our God?"

If church has become a bit tedious, it is probably a sign that things in your soul life are not quite right...

These people of God in this time have lost all their daily requirements for life. The food and drinks have been suddenly taken away with the onslaught of the hoard of locusts. The cupboards are stripped bare and there is nothing to eat.

Just like the temporal food, they have also lost the joy and gladness in the house of God. When we lose our daily bread, we can often lose interest in the bread of life also. When times are hard, we can find ourselves losing interest in the things of God and becoming lazy about our spiritual duties, and the things we once loved fade away. For these people, they have allowed the blessings of life to distract them from the Lord and so they are fallen away.

The people truly have lost everything for they have lost their joy in the Lord, which is their strength and their motivation to dwell in the house of the Lord has gone. Their Christian assurance has dried up and they are fallen away. It is almost like they are not the people of God any longer but have reverted to worldliness and therefore the ensuing woe and unhappiness.

They are miserable because God is against them and has allowed this intense suffering, so now they are turning away from Him and have lost their peace in His presence.

Beloved, let use learn to stick closely with the Lord. Only in him do we have life and peace, joy and gladness, forgiveness and mercy in all our troubles. Let us not be dragged down by the trials we face and lose our joy through carelessness and unbelief.

V17 Rot

"The seeds rot under their clods. The granaries are laid desolate. The barns are broken down, for the grain has withered."

The crops are gone. The produce, the growth and the seeds have rotted in the ground, so there will be no other possibility for a harvest.

If the people are to be saved it will be by the hand of the Lord alone.

"...for by grace you have been saved through faith, and that not of yourselves; it is the gift of God.."

Ephesians 2:4

It is exactly the same for us today. Before we come to Christ there is not even the seed of saving faith in our lives, but only sinfulness, selfishness and hostility towards the Lord. There must be a work of God's amazing grace in our hearts, minds and souls if we are to be saved. We must acquiesce. We need to repent of our ways and succumb to the love and mercy of the only Saviour of our souls. Jesus has paid the price already and all we have to do is trust in Him and what He has done for us. It is so easy, and yet so difficult for us to give in to Him.

Beloved, all we have is sin and death, but Christ or Lord offers us life and peace. Let us embrace Him and all that He offers to us in His mighty love. He will bring the harvest out of the desolation in our souls and give us spiritual life. His ways are ways of pleasantness, and all His paths are peace...

V18 Groan

"How the animals groan! The herds of livestock are perplexed, because they have no pasture. Yes, the flocks of sheep are made desolate."

The attention now turns to the animals who are affected by the famine. The misdeeds of the people have had an effect on everything. The animals also have nothing to eat or drink and are made desolate by the effects of the famine. The consequences of our sin run deep, not just for ourselves but for others as well. The things we do and say affect those around us and can cause a spiritual famine in our families, communities and countries. We are experiencing this in the West today, as so many have turned from following the Lord and are following false teachers and fables.

The sheep of the pasture of the Lord are made desolate by the falsehoods and many are suffering great loss in the inner life of their soul. The people of God are not being fed good nourishing spiritual food and are therefore dying in the pews. The Lord must come down and save us, for we perish... we dig for food, but it is hard to find.

The people of God are waiting for the return of their Saviour and cry out to Him for deliverance. The whole creation is groaning and suffering waiting for the deliverance of the children of God and the new creation wherein dwells righteousness.

"For the creation waits with eager expectation for the children of God to be revealed. For the creation was subjected to vanity, not of its own will, but because of him who subjected it, in hope that the creation itself also will be delivered from the bondage of decay into the liberty of the glory of the children of God. For we know that the whole creation groans and travails in pain together until now."

Romans 8:19-22

One day soon the groaning will cease, and all shall be peace in the kingdom of God. All evil will be gone. All want and needs will be met, and joy and peace will reign. This is the glorious hope of the people of God and a motivation to turn for all sin and be ready when the Lord returns for us. We do not need to be desolate, for we have this glorious hope which is true and certain.

V19 Cry

"Lord, I cry to you, For the fire has devoured the pastures of the wilderness, and the flame has burned all the trees of the field."

In the midst of the destitution and disaster, this is the only thing that we can do and the most powerful thing we can do. We cry to the Lord in our pains and troubles, and He will deliver us. The trouble here, is the influx of hoard of locusts that have destroyed everything and are likened to a devouring fire that has burned up all the pasture land and the trees of the field. Fire totally destroys and there is no possibility of getting the constituent part back as they were before. It is wholly destructive, and this has been the judgment of the Lord on the sin of the people.

God will not tolerate sin, especially in is beloved people, and will deal with us and help us to "see" the rottenness that we have fallen into and give us a way out in repentance.

The problem with these people that the prophet is ministering to, is that they are almost insensible to the voice of the Lord. They do not listen to the prophet. They do not cry out in their famine. They are less sensible than the beasts which have cried to the Lord for food and sustenance. Now the mountains and cool wildernesses are burned up and destroyed and still they do not cry out.

The prophet says that he alone will cry to the Lord. It is a personal response to the situation and Joel recognises his need for the Lord, as do the animals and the field. The people remain deaf to the pleadings of the Lord. They cannot even respond to the trial of fire. This is the natural state of the human heart without God, and a desperately sad and depraved one.

Beloved, may we cry out in our need and experience the deliverance of the Lord before the trial get too onerous and we really fall and fail. May we see the warning signs in our own lives that we are wandering and stop the slipping before it gets away from the presence of the Lord.

"Be merciful to me, God, be merciful to me, for my soul takes refuge in you. Yes, in the shadow of your wings, I will take refuge, until disaster has passed. I cry out

to God Most High, to God who
accomplishes my requests for me."

Psalm 57:1-2

Those who call out to Him are never
disappointed and He will deliver the
humble from the temptation, the snare
and the destruction that await those who
refuse. These people in this time of Joel
are in deep trouble and their hearts are far
from the Lord. They refuse to cry...

V20 Pant

"Yes, the animals of the field pant to you, for the water brooks have dried up, And the fire has devoured the pastures of the wilderness."

The prophet Joel hits home the problem. Even the animals are more sensible to their need than the people of God. All streams and water holes have dried up and the animals are thirsty. They pant to the Lord, longing for his blessing and provision. The people are not so...

Those who seek the Lord go after Him with a true and full heart of love for Him. They desire Him above all other things.

"As the deer pants for the water brooks, so my soul pants after you, God."

Psalm 42:1

As an animal seek provision from the Lord, so also do we. We long for Him and are desperate for His felt presence and provision for our empty souls. These people in Joel's time, do not. May we be wise and love the Lord our God with every fibre of our being.

Joel Chapter Two

32 Verses

Joel Chapter Two

V1 Alarm

"Blow the trumpet in Zion, and sound an alarm in my holy mountain! Let all the inhabitants of the land tremble, for the day of the Lord comes, for it is close at hand:"

The people of God are asleep and insensible to what is coming against them. They do not see nor read the signs in the circumstances of life, and so the trumpet of God will sound against them from the holy hill of Zion, the place where God dwells. As the priests sound the trumpet to call the people to repentance, so the trumpet of God is sounded at the coming tragedy, not of locusts, but of final and irrevocable judgment. It is not a trumpet of rejoicing but of wild alarm. It is to awaken the people and warn them of the coming doom, the impending day that will bring judgment and sorrow on them, for they are lost and without hope of salvation.

They have slept away their chances and have not been faithful to the Lord or paid attention to the warning He has sent them, so now they face the day of His great wrath with no Saviour to mediate for them. They are in the worst possible state.

The mention here in this verse of the day of the Lord, refers not just to the tragedy of the destruction of the locusts and the famine they bring, but the day of reckoning when the souls of the people will be judged. The day has now come, a day in the future when all will give account for the deeds done in the body. The great day of his wrath is coming, and the judgment will be poured out, not in love but in great anger against all the enemies of God, who reject His holy laws and the provision of His salvation offered to all people.

"Neither their silver nor their gold will be able to deliver them in the day of the Lord's wrath, but the whole land will be devoured by the fire of his jealousy; for he will make an end, yes, a terrible end, of all those who dwell in the land."

Zephaniah 1:18

The day of the Lord will surely come, as the other days that were foretold by the prophets. There will be no recompense on the last great day, but all will face their judgment and the Lord will make an end to all evil and evil doers.

V2 Spreading

"A day of darkness and gloominess, a day of clouds and thick darkness. As the dawn spreading on the mountains, a great and strong people; there has never been the like, neither will there be any more after them, even to the years of many generations."

The day of the Lord will not be a happy day for those who are under its judgment. The day is coming for these wayward people, and it will come in the form of a huge swarm of locusts. It will appear as a day of thick darkness, there will be so many of them. The sun and daylight will be blotted out for there has never been such a hoard of marauders such as these.

They will appear like the sun coming up over the mountains and spreading across the countryside so fast and furiously. As the light travels so fast, so will these destructive hoard of insects. There has never been such a swarm as this one – never been so many insects like these who will destroy everything in front of them. Neither will there ever be again, for they are the judgment of the Lord, like the final judgement that is to come.

They are described here as *"strong people,"* like a marauding army of invaders from over the mountains who will sweep in like the sea and drown all the land with their plague. They will spread like light over the ground as it arrives over the mountains. No one will be able to stop it, for it will sweep away everything in sight.

We can only imagine the terror at the sight of this monstrous and destructive army cascading over the hills and devouring the work and livelihoods of the people. They watch helpless as the army of locusts eat their way through the entire land in a few hours. They leave destitution and famine and death. It surely is a day of gloominess, and the prophet is right to bemoan the trouble of the people, even if they do not see it for themselves. They must call out to the Lord to deliver them, for there is no one else who can possibly help.

Beloved, when the day of the Lord comes for us, may we be ready to meet it under the shadow of the wings of the Almighty God, who will shelter His people from the last great storm and bring all His ransomed people home safely and triumphant. May we be among that great throng and look in confidence and rest at that last battle where the enemies of the Lord, and of His people, will finally and forever be vanquished.

"I saw the heaven opened, and behold, a white horse, and he who sat on it is called Faithful and True. In righteousness he judges and makes war. His eyes are a flame of fire, and on his head are many crowns. He has names written and a name written which no one knows but he himself. He is clothed in a garment sprinkled with blood. His name is called "The Word of God." The armies which are in heaven followed him on white horses, clothed in white, pure, fine linen. Out of his mouth proceeds a sharp, double-edged sword, that with it he should strike the nations. He will rule them with an iron rod. He treads the winepress of the fierceness of the wrath of God, the Almighty. He has on his garment and on his thigh a name written, "KING OF KINGS, AND LORD OF LORDS."

Revelation 19:11-16

V3 Devours

"A fire devours before them, and behind them, a flame burns. The land is as the garden of Eden before them, and behind them, a desolate wilderness. Yes, and no one has escaped them."

Fire is the most destructive element, for it changes the substance of things irrevocably. It destroys completely with no hope of renewal. These locusts will destroy like the fire. They will consume everything before them and leave nothing but charred remains of embers behind them. The land is bountiful for it is the land God gave to his people and is a veritable garden of Eden with plenty for all, but it will be reduced to wasteland – a desolate wilderness of no use to human or animal.

These creatures devour. This is their goal and reason for existence. They must grow and live and so they eat all before them to nourish their own lives at the expense of everything else. They are like fire that totally devours and cannot be stopped. They are a curse, for they take and never give.

This is the outcome for all who forget God and refuse His many offers of mercy. Lives will be devoured by the wastefulness of the locust and destroyed by the deceitfulness of sin. The prophet continues to warn the people, but so far it has fallen on deaf ears. They want sound bites of comfort and love and not the searching power of the Holy Spirit. They want the temporal blessings of this life and not the reality of the spiritual blessings in their Lord.

Beloved, may this not be true of us, but may we seek the Lord with all our hearts and keep our pathway pure, that we might escape His searching trials that will find us unable to stand up under them.

"To You, O Lord, I Lift Up My Soul. My God, I have trusted in you. Don't let me be shamed. Don't let my enemies triumph over me. Yes, no one who waits for you shall be shamed. They shall be shamed who deal treacherously without cause. Show me your ways, O Lord, Teach me your paths."

Psalm 25:1-4

V4 Horsemen

"The appearance of them is as the appearance of horses, and as horsemen, so do they run."

Once horses are running there is no stopping them, like a stampede that cannot be brought to a halt for any reason. This is a powerful analogy for the prophet Joel to use, since horses are powerful animals and used for warfare and hard labour. The bolt of the horses from the starting stalls at the beginning of a race is unstoppable. Wild horses thunder down the hills at break-neck speed, exalting in their freedom. Horses that run into battle are equally powerful and are trained to be bold and strong in the face of great danger. It was not for no reason that armies of old used them for speed and their intimidating qualities!

This is like the locusts that pour over the land like liquid and touch every nook and cranny of the landscape, filling it with their power and their dread. As a charging army with men on horseback that drive the animals into the thick of the battle, where the fight is the hottest and the most virulent, so these locusts will install fear into all that seek to stand against them.

They run.

"I listened and heard, but they didn't speak aright: no man repents him of his wickedness, saying, What have I done? everyone turns to his course, as a horse that rushes headlong in the battle."

Jeremiah 8:6

Wickedness and oppression run like horses into the battle. Souls of the wicked sin without conscience and excuse their behaviour. They run over the land and strip it bare of righteousness and justice and put in its place destitution and spiritual famine. This is happening all over our world, and we can but watch and see the destruction of our societies. Like Great War-horses, the sins of the people spread like wildfire, like locusts over the land. No one can stop them except the intervening hand of God, and He will, to rescue His believed people and bring many souls to righteousness.

"We looked for peace, but no good came; [and] for a time of healing, and behold,

---

dismay! The snorting of his horses is heard from Dan: at the sound of the neighing of his strong ones the whole land trembles; for they are come, and have devoured the land and all that is in it; the city and those who dwell therein."

Jeremiah 8:15-16

It is a common theme of the prophets and should fill us with concern. The Lord sends trouble to teach us and speaks to us in our troubles. May we listen and turn and be saved.

V5 Leap

"Like the noise of chariots on the tops of the mountains do they leap, like the noise of a flame of fire that devours the stubble, as a strong people set in battle array."

The armies of the locusts are ready to descend and destroy. We can hear the noise of them, the chariots on the tops of the hills, clanging and champing to be away into the fight. Then roar of the wheels as they descend with such vigour into the valley of death. Such will be the situation in that last battle against the Lord and His anointed king, the Lord Jesus Christ. The chariots will leap with the vehemence of the hatred against God and His people, but to no avail.

The sound will be like the roar of fire as it takes hold of the dry wasteland and devours all ahead of it. The fire will flame out into the country and leap and crackle until all is consumed. These pictures are very powerful for we can relate to them in our lives. If we have seen great fire, then we will know how it takes hold and incinerates the whole edifice of a building. The flames leap and crash and roar until nothing is left. Once it takes hold, nothing or no one can stop it.

We have another picture of a great people, strong and mighty to fight in the battle and arrayed as a huge army on the tops of the hills ready for the word to advance. They are kitted out with armour and armaments and are ready for the fight to the death. They are cruel and filled with hate. They will destroy just for the sake of doing it and are set in full battle array against the people of God. We will see them one day soon and will be also arrayed with the Lord Jesus in robes of white, on white horses of the saints of God.

There will be no fighting, nor do the people of God carry weapons. Christ on the white charger will destroy them all with the Word from his mouth. The enemies of Christ can never stand against Him nor succeed.

"The beast was taken, and with him the false prophet who worked the signs in his sight, with which he deceived those who had received the mark of the beast and those who worshiped his image. These two were thrown alive into the lake of fire that

burns with sulphur. The rest were killed with the sword of him who sat on the horse, the sword which came forth out of his mouth. All the birds were filled with their flesh."

Revelation 19:20-21

No matter how destructive the enemies might seem to us, they can never touch us or steal the glory of the people of God. We ensure we are on the side of the right armies, the Army of the Lord of Hosts...

V6 Pale

"At their presence the peoples are in anguish. All faces have grown pale."

The horror of the situation had finally sunk in. These marauders will stop human life in its tracks and there will be death and judgment for certain from the arrival of these unwanted invaders. Like the attack of an occupying army, they will strip all bare and rape and pillage the land of all living greenery.

The people are finally seeing their fate and are in anguish about the future. The blood drains from their skin and they experience real and terrible dread. They are finally seeing what the prophet had been telling them and the warnings he has spoken that have fallen on deaf ears, are now heeded, but it is too late.

"She is empty, void, and waste. The heart melts, the knees knock together, their bodies and faces have grown pale."

Nahum 2:10

Some translations translate the face that grows pale, as growing in darkness, a sign of impending death. Altogether it is a dreadful scene as people realise too late that they have rejected the warnings and now face the unthinkable consequences.

V7 Climb

"They run like mighty men. They climb the wall like warriors. They each march in his line, and they don't swerve off course."

This army is strong and completely disciplined. They are swift and relentless. Like warriors who can run like the wind with great power and speed, they arrive over the mountains and hit the cities with such overwhelming might. They are not kept out by the city walls but scale them so easily and over-run the buildings. They are like super-trained athletes that never give up and nothing stops their ceaseless advances.

Every member of this army is supremely suited to their task. They keep in line with military precision and never deviate from the inner orders within them. They know exactly what to do and do it ruthlessly and with speed and persistence. They have no leader, but the inner voice of instinct drives them forward bravely.

"The locusts have no king, yet they advance in ranks."
Proverbs 30:27

These insects know exactly what they are doing and keep to the inner disciple with great precision. It is what makes them feared and consistent in what they do. Like the locusts in Egypt, they infiltrate every house and steal everything they can find. They can scale every wall and no amount of protection can keep them out.

"Your houses shall be filled, and the houses of all your servants, and the houses of all the Egyptians; as neither your fathers nor your fathers' fathers have seen, since the day that they were on the earth to this day.'" He turned, and went out from Pharaoh."

Exodus 10:6

This is a plague of plagues, and a sight to behold.

Perhaps we can learn from the locusts and learn from their military discipline that they show in these great events. Maybe we can learn from the inner working of the Spirit within us and be obedient to His promptings and give our all to our Lord and God. This is what He expects from us and we give it willingly.

V8 March

"Neither does one jostle another; they march everyone in his path, and they burst through the defences, and don't break ranks."

Iron discipline in the inner beings of these mighty insects, causes their progress to be swift and certain.

They never break ranks or get in the way of each other, for each knows its place in the scheme of the army. Every one of the individuals has their place and their task in the great army, and they all carry out their tasks with ruthless success. They march in unison and overcome the defences that are set up against them, because of their discipline and persistence. They never step out of line and never set themselves against each other.

We can learn much from their iron discipline and their ability to march straight and true to the purpose of the whole body of insects. They do not interfere with each other's progress and keep to the purpose set out for them as individuals in the huge group.

We are the body of Christ and should also be concerned to carry out our tasks in the will of God and for His glory and not our own. We work together as the body of Christ and are cared for an individuals, and as part of that glorious body of the Lord Jesus as our head and Lord. This army of locust is successful because it is obedient to the corporate purpose, and we also will conquer sin in the name of Christ and for his glory and our eternal good.

"... that you may walk worthily of the Lord, to please him in all respects, bearing fruit in every good work, and increasing in the knowledge of God; strengthened with all power, according to the might of his glory, for all endurance and perseverance with joy; giving thanks to the Father, who made us fit to be partakers of the inheritance of the saints in light;"

Colossians 1:10-12

V9 Thieves

"They rush on the city. They run on the wall. They climb up into the houses. They enter in at the windows like thieves."

The strategy of this army is very straightforward. They conquer through their great number and their ability to infiltrate every nook and cranny of the invaded city. The locusts rush on the city and hit it like a mighty flood and spill over into all the houses and windows. They fly in and over run the whole environment, stripping it of anything they can eat and rendering it useless for human habitation.

These marauders cannot be kept out with armaments or systems of defence that humans have come up with. The locusts are triumphant in their conquest and climb into the very lives of the people like thieves. They are unstoppable and take to themselves everything of value that will sustain their life and consume all green vegetation.

These insects will sweep over the city and strip it completely bare. They leave nothing of value and take all that will be useful in the lives of its inhabitants. They are the ultimate thieves, for they leave nothing behind them, only devastation and desert.

"... they are more than the locusts and are innumerable."

Jeremiah 46:23

The armies of total destruction are described as a hoard of locusts who strip away all life support. They are the judgment of the Lord and do His bidding.

V10 Tremble

"The earth quakes before them. The heavens tremble. The sun and the moon are darkened, and the stars withdraw their shining."

This is a further indication of this event being the judgment of God as it affects the daylight, the sun and moon and the stars. This arrival of the locusts is a precursor for judgment and is reminiscent of the last great day. It spells out terror as in the opening of the sixth seal.

"I saw when he opened the sixth seal, and there was a great earthquake. The sun became black as sackcloth made of hair, and the whole moon became as blood."

Revelation 6:12

It is a sign of the end times and the coming of a certain day of judgment that will bring total disaster for those under its dominion. It is a frightening time with earthquakes, heavenly disturbances, lack of light and even the stars do not shine. It will bring terror to the people of earth and the coming Day of the Lord.

The Lord never leaves us without knowledge. He speaks to us in His Word and gives warning to the unbeliever and comfort to His people. We rejoice to know such a God and His great love for us. He will not let the present sinful situation be prolonged, but will come again in righteousness, justice and mercy.

We should tremble before Him and find salvation in the only Saviour, the Lord Jesus Christ lest we find ourselves trembling on that terrible day, unforgiven and with no refuge from the judgment. He still reaches out in mercy to those who will repent and believe.

V11 Awesome

"The Lord thunders his voice before his army; for his forces are very great; for he is strong who obeys his command; for the day of the Lord is great and very awesome, and who can endure it?"

The language here does not just apply to this present judgment that the people of God are going through in the days of Joel, but it synonymous with the last great Day of the Lord. The enemies of the Lord will surely gather against Him but will not stand. The power of the Lord is demonstrated in the thundering of His voice as He announces the presence of His great army, the redeemed people of the Lord. The Word of the Lord stands supreme over everything and every scenario. He had the first word in the building of the earth, and He will have the last word in the destruction of His handiwork.

Those who obey the Lord are strong, because they obey the Word of the Lord which does not fail. This Day of reckoning is coming soon and no one who stands against the Lord shall in any way prevail. The rhetorical question adds power to the statements. *"Who shall endure it?"* The answer is certain and obvious, for we are talking about the mighty God, the maker of heavens and earth, and the sovereign God over everything and every being that exists. No one can endure who challenges Him and His eternal majesty.

The Scripture stands supreme over the created order, the passage of time and the life of every human that has ever existed. No one can stand against Him, and His word will finally and totally prevail. All who refuse Him will be judged and all who love Him will be exalted. Why wait for the thundering of His voice, for He yet calls out to us in love.

"Come to me, all you who labour and are heavily burdened, and I will give you rest."

Matthew 11:28

V12 Even now

"Yet even now," says the Lord, "turn to me with all your heart, and with fasting, and with weeping, and with mourning."

Even now at the last minute, the offer of mercy still stands. The day of the Lord is almost upon the people, but there is still opportunity to repent. They must turn with all their heart and mean what they say and stick to it. There must be no wavering as they realise their sinfulness and turn away from it. They testify to their truthfulness and sincerity with weeping, fasting and great mourning. Are we also on the threshold of judgment? Still God calls to us to repent and come to Him and He will freely pardon us.

The pathway to peace is free and the forgiveness is full, but we must be sincere. There must be no turning back and looking back like the wife of Lot, in the Old Testament, who turned in regret at leaving Sodom and was turned into a pillar of salt. We do not regret leaving our sin but leave it feely and fully with glad hearts that we are redeemed people and can have the liberty of Christ and the power of the Holy

Spirit in us, to help us fight temptation and the fear of failure.

How will we know we are sincere? We do not turn back. We do not go back to our old ways and find ourselves imbibing the way of sinfulness again. Repentance is so difficult for us, for our hearts hold us fast in the hardness of the moral disease of sin and don't want to let go of our pleasures.

We falsely think we will be miserable in following the Lord and our enemy tells us that God is a spoil sport, and we know better than He does, what is good for us. We cannot see that God has greater and better things stored up for His people, even in this life! There are better things for the Christian and every "loss" is a gain in the kingdom of God. Our problem is we do not actually hate our sin but want to cling onto it. Only Christ within can break this bond...

V13 Tear your heart

"Tear your heart, and not your garments, and turn to the Lord, your God; for he is gracious and merciful, slow to anger, and abundant in loving kindness, and relents from sending calamity."

The Lord requires true repentance. We can be good at the outward show of penitence yet remain unrepentant. The people of Joel's day were so far from the Lord that they couldn't seem to reach a place of sincerity and the Lord is telling them that He sees through their outward show. Torn clothing was a sign of deep sorrow, but easy to imitate for an audience! God requires more than that.

Torn hearts are the real sign of repentance. We must be devastated about our sin so that we never countenance it again. It is too easy to presume on forgiveness and that overall, we are doing well, but we harbour sin, especially sins that cannot be seen. The heart sins are what really bring us down and separate us from the Lord.

Petty jealousies and hatreds towards others and sins that we think are acceptable and understandable are in no way acceptable to the Lord. God will not tolerate any sin in His people because He knows that it takes us away for Him and makes us more and more world orientated. We need the Lord and only Him and all the rest will be added to us as we need it.

The Lord gives us time and opportunity to turn, and we must take it seriously. He is slow to anger, but we must not presume on that. His lovingkindness is beyond our understanding, and we must honour Him and not take His patience for granted. The people have gone a long way down the road of perdition, but God waits for them to turn and He will pardon them, even at this late time.

"Let the wicked forsake his way, and the unrighteous man his thoughts; and let him return to the Lord, and he will have mercy on him; and to our God, for he will abundantly pardon."

Isaiah 55:7

V14 Offering

"Who knows? He may turn and relent, and leave a blessing behind him, even a meal offering and a drink offering to the Lord, your God."

The prophet Joel seems to interject an element of doubt about the offer of mercy. This is to ensure that the repentance of the people is right and good and to encourage them to seek the Lord now at this time of the offer of mercy. They need to act now and secure their salvation and not put it off or wallow in self-pity any longer. They are in an extremely dangerous place and are on the brink of starvation and famine, and yet they are wavering. Their souls are teetering on the brink of eternity, and they procrastinate!

The prophet encourages them that God will leave them a blessing and not punishment. God seeks to dwell and commune with His people through the offerings at the temple and they may yet enjoy that privilege with Him. The punishment seems so certain, but there is yet time to turn and heal their land.

"...for he says, "At an acceptable time I listened to you, in a day of salvation I helped you." Behold, now is the acceptable time. Behold, now is the day of salvation."

2 Corinthians 6:2

V15 Solemn

"Blow the trumpet in Zion! Sanctify a fast. Call a solemn assembly."

The warning must go out. The people must hear the final deal. They must know the danger they are in and not walk blindfolded into the wrath of God. There must be the public proclamation of the gospel so that all can have the opportunity to hear. It must be loud and strong like the trumpet sounding a clear note of attention so that no one misses their opportunity to repent and turn from their wickedness.

"For if the trumpet gave an uncertain sound, who would prepare himself for war?"

1 Corinthians 14:8

The trumpet calls the people a solemn and sacred gathering. This is the most serious of assemblies to gather the hearts of the people to the Lord. There is to be fasting, to focus the mind on the seriousness of this situation for the whole Israelites nation. This is a public and national expression of guilt and confession of sin, that it may be forgiven and covered over by the mercy of God.

In our day, surely the trumpet sounds an uncertain sound. We pray that God will raise up those who will proclaim the gospel in all its power and glory to a dying culture. We are on the same road as these Israelites in the prophet Joel's day, and stand at a precipice of doom, though we don't know it, for we are anaesthetised to our need and our danger. Beloved, let us all awaken and share the good news of Jesus Christ to the dying world and rescue many from the darkness. Let us be bold and courageous for the sake of Christ and the people who will perish without Him.

V16 Gather

"Gather the people. Sanctify the assembly. Assemble the elders. Gather the children, and those who nurse from breasts. Let the bridegroom go forth from his room, and the bride out of her room."

Everyone is to be gathered in that whole nation assembly. The prophet is instructed that the priests sanctify the people and assemble the leaders with them. This event is for everyone, and all the nation must be gathered together in solidarity with what they are doing. The old must be there, since they should know better than to descend into the dissolute lifestyle that the nation has imbibed. They are doubly to blame for the state of the nation, for they have age and wisdom on their side. The leaders also and especially the religious leaders, have gone so badly astray that they have let the people go to ruin. They will be judged more severely for their remiss attitudes.

Even the children and nursing babies must be there that they might witness the mercy of God in the repentance of His people. This is a state of national mourning and repentance and must be inclusive of every soul. The wrath of God is over the whole society including the beasts of the field. God holds them all culpable and will not exonerate any without repentance.

Those who have events to go to, even weddings, must leave them and attend this national event. Everyone leaves their pleasures to attend to this pressing state of sorrow. It is inappropriate to enjoy the finer things in life, when all is lost for the people of God. Too many enjoy the fruits of sinful lives and do not mourn the state of the church and its weak and ineffectual state in our world. We countenance sin and cover over the judgment that awaits with feasting and enjoyment for ourselves.

V17 Heritage

"Let the priests, the ministers of the Lord, weep between the porch and the altar, and let them say, "Spare your people, Lord, and don't give your heritage to reproach, that the nations should rule over them. Why should they say among the peoples, 'Where is their God?'"

The first people in line for the weeping are the ministers and priest of the Lord. They have been so remiss they have allowed the people to slip into sin with no reproof. They cannot approach the Lord, nor can they go to the altar, for they are unworthy priests. They must stay in the congregation of the people and weep with the people, so all can see their tears and realise the depth of the problem. They have lost their privileges because of their sin. God tells them what to say, for they are so remiss that have forgotten how to approach the Lord and how to repent. They are to come to God with sober minds and torn hearts and remonstrate with Him and present their case for forgiveness. Why should God wait and forgive any longer?

"Come now, and let us reason together," *says the Lord: "Though your sins be as* *scarlet, they shall be as white as snow.* *Though they be red like crimson, they* *shall be as wool."*

Isaiah 1:18

The kindness and the mercy of the Lord always shines through. The sins of the people are deep dyed, but God waits for them to come to Him and present their case against wrath. God will listen and though they are sinful, yet there is forgiveness and the offer of cleansing.

The priests argue that the people of God will become a reproach to the unbelieving world if they are chastised, and the name of God will be derided by the enemies of God. This is a probability, but God will not be deflected from justice because of that consideration. This is another consequence the people have not considered that the enemies of God will scoff and rejoice at their demise. God is dishonoured by their behaviour, and they have not considered Him. The priests and ministers are to plead the case with the Lord.

"Answer me, Lord, for your loving kindness is good. According to the multitude of your tender mercies, turn to me. Don't hide your face from your servant, for I am in distress. Answer me speedily! Draw near to my soul, and redeem it. Ransom me because of my enemies."

Psalm 69:16-18

This is an appropriate prayer for the repentant soul, full of pleading with the Lord and a heartfelt desire for forgiveness and mercy. We seek redemption and the ransom of our souls from the cruelty of the enemy.

V18 Pity

*"Then the Lord was jealous for his land,
And had pity on his people."*

The pleas of the priests are heard by the
Lord, and He listens to their cry for mercy
and grace. God does not change His mind,
but in His forbearance is showing us His
dedication to justice and will always give
way to mercy.

"Mercy triumphs over judgment."

James 2:13

There are many mysteries in the Scripture
and many aspects of God's character we
do not understand, but we know He is the
sovereign Lord, and He decides to relent
or punish the guilty. The pleadings of the
prophet are heard by the people, and they
now turn. The people and their leaders
and the whole nation repents before the
Lord and the wrath of God passes and He
forgives the sin of the people. The Lord is
full of pity for the creatures He has made
and will turn from His wrath at their
pleadings, if sincere.

The Lord is also jealous of His people and will not hand them over to the judgment of the wicked without mercy. He is jealous that they should not suffer the ignominy of going into destitution, even though they deserve it. He will not bring judgment on His land unless there is no repentance.

"You have heard of the patience of Job, and have seen the Lord in the outcome, and how the Lord is full of compassion and mercy."

James 5:11

The pity of the Lord has saved His people from certain destruction. The Lord softens their heart to believe, and they turn and are saved. So also with us. When we hear God speak into our mind and conscience, may we repent and put all our trust in Him.

V19 Satisfied

"The Lord answered his people, "Behold, I will send you grain, new wine, and oil, and you will be satisfied with them; and I will no more make you a reproach among the nations."

The justice of the Lord is slow to strike, and His mercy is quick to bless. The people of God have turned and been forgiven, and they know this because the Lord now promises to bless them. The Lord will remove the reproach of His people and renew their vigour before the nations. He will not require them to be constantly regaled and looked upon as pariahs but rescue them from the blaming gaze of the ungodly nations around them.

The gross sins of the people of God have been atoned for, and God is willing to forgive them all their moral debt and set them free to live and serve Him in great joy. He will pour in the oil and the wine of blessing and healing and give the grain of sustenance for the fainting hearts of the nation.

This is the gracious answer of the Lord to a sinful and destitute people, who are His people, whom He loves. The Lord is kind to the unlovely and saves those who are in peril of death. He loves to be kind and to exercise His mercy and compassion to the broken hearted. The Israelites nation has severely tested His patience, and has tried His grace sorely, but repentance brings salvation and healing to the nation. It is the same for us also. We fall into sin and get caught up in persistent wrong-doing and cannot get free of it. It holds us like a vice and we are trapped in the sin of our hearts and minds. Only the mercy of the Lord can free us from the grip of sin and bring us to the state of repentance and faith.

When we come to Him, we accept the remedy for our sin, the sacrifice of Jesus on the cross and the price He so willingly paid to set us free. The path of humility is the only way. There is no other Saviour, and we can never save ourselves. We throw ourselves on the mercy of the Lord and we are safe to do so, for He will fully pardon us.

"... *let the wicked forsake his way, and the unrighteous man his thoughts; and let him return to the Lord, and he will have mercy on him; and to our God, for he will abundantly pardon."*

Isaiah 55:7

Only the death of Christ could satisfy the demand of God's holy law and He has fulfilled all righteousness for our sake. Only God can deal with us and forgive us and satisfy our weary hearts and save our wretched souls. This is what He did for His people, and He will do for us when we also repent and believe.

V20 Remove

"But I will remove the northern army far away from you, and will drive it into a barren and desolate land, its front into the eastern sea, and its back into the western sea; and its stench will come up, and its bad smell will rise." Surely he has done great things."

The Lord continues to bless His people with release from their enemies and promises to remove the threat and the reality of the locust invasion for good. The locust army is referred to as the northern army for it is just like a band of marauders that are threatening the land and will invade and destroy all around it. This army has been waiting in the wings of the scenario for the command of the Lord to exercise His judgment on the nation. Now the repentance has happened, and salvation has come there is no need for this invasion.

God promises to remove the threat far away from His people and this army will now be driven into the destitution it threatened on the people of God. It will be drowned in the depths of the sea never to be remembered any more except for the momentary rank smell it will make as it is disposed of. This is reminiscent of the promise to cast our sins into the sea of God's forgetfulness, never to be remembered any more.

"He will again have compassion on us. He will tread our iniquities under foot; and you will cast all their sins into the depths of the sea."

Micah 7:19

Surely, He has done great things! The Lord is merciful toward His people and loves them and rescues them from their sin and condemnation. The whole of the people of God are saved and not one is lost...

V21 Rejoice

"Land, don't be afraid. Be glad and rejoice, for the Lord has done great things."

The Lord exalts in His people and rejoices with them. He tells them not to be afraid any longer for all punishment and wrath has now passed away. He Himself has dealt with the problem and the disgrace has passed over. The people can now rejoice for the judgment has gone and they are rescued from it. The whole land can be glad for the desolation has been averted and the land is now free.

The Lord has done great things in rescuing His people. Such is the work of salvation that has been procured for them. Never again will they face this condemnation for it has all passed away.

"There is therefore now no condemnation to those who are in Christ Jesus, who don't walk according to the flesh, but according to the Spirit."

Romans 8:1

The people have returned to the Lord and are now living in fellowship with Him and can enjoy all the benefits of their salvation. We also can enjoy the presence of the Lord with us when we repent and give up our sin and deny the flesh and its hold on our lives. To live in the power of the Spirit of God is life and peace.

"For the mind of the flesh is death, but the mind of the Spirit is life and peace;"

Romans 8:6

When we walk with our God the Lord, it makes us joyful because we are in his gracious presence and at peace with Him. To entertain the flesh is to dampen that relationship and cause ourselves a lot of grief. We do not need to live in doubt or fear but in the freedom that comes when we acquiesce to the love of Christ and obey Him.

V22 Strength

"Don't be afraid, you animals of the field; for the pastures of the wilderness spring up, for the tree bears its fruit. The fig tree and the vine yield their strength."

The judgment has passed and there is no need of fear, even for the animals in the fields, who were also affected by the sinful behaviour and lifestyle of the people. God speaks to them and tells them that there is plenty for them all. The pastures are springing up out of the wilderness and the trees are coming into fruit. The fig tree and the vine are becoming rampant for they have regained their strength.

This is synonymous with the blessings of the people of God. Where before they wandered in the wilderness, they are now enjoying the green pastures of their own land. The growth of the ground has sprung up to furnish all their needs and desires and they are walking in the green pastures.

"The Lord is my shepherd: I shall lack nothing. He makes me lie down in green pastures. He leads me beside still waters.

He restores my soul. He guides me in the paths of righteousness for his name's sake."

Psalm 23:1-3

The people of God now enjoy safe pasture for the Day of Wrath is passed and they are safe in the land. Their lives are bearing fruit to God and are enjoying the strength of the Spirit within. This is true for their lives in this world and also for the life to come when Christ returns to take His people to heaven. We have freedom and power now to live for God and will enter into the full reality of that kingdom life when Christ comes for His church.

"I heard a loud voice out of heaven saying, "Behold, God's dwelling is with people, and he will dwell with them, and they will be his people, and God himself will be with them as their God. He will wipe away every tear from their eyes. Death will be no more; neither will there be mourning, nor crying, nor pain, any more. The first things have passed away."

Revelation 21:3-4

V23 Rain

"Be glad then, you children of Zion, and rejoice in the Lord, your God; for he gives you the former rain in just measure, and he causes the rain to come down for you, the former rain and the latter rain, as before."

God will pour out such blessing on His people that they will rejoice. As He rejoices over their salvation, so we can also rejoice at what the Lord has done on our behalf. Salvation is ours, never to be lost, for it does not depend on our performance, but on the grace of God. God has sent the rain as blessing on His people, that their land will be green and verdant and fruitful. God blesses us and gives us thankfulness, that we also might serve Him and rejoice to do His perfect will. Our lives will then produce fruit for eternity, and we will have peace.

The rain of the gospel falls when the Lord designs it to fall. It falls in both seasons of the year that there might be fruit to God all the year. As the message of the gospel goes forward, we share it in faith that it will bear fruit and souls will be saved. God sends the blessing of the past year and the year to come. All blessing is from His gracious hand and will sustain us in all the circumstances of our lives. We are commanded to rejoice, we should rejoice for all things are ours, the gift of God, and we enjoy the blessings with great thankfulness and joy.

We thank Him for the blessing of the *"former and the latter rain,"* the rain that falls at the beginning of life and the rain that falls on our later years. The Lord will never leave His children unfruitful and without purpose. He does not leave us wondering what it is all about but gives us usefulness and purpose in all our circumstances.

"...that Christ may dwell in your hearts through faith; to the end that you, being rooted and grounded in love, may be strengthened to comprehend with all the saints what is the breadth and length and height and depth, and to know Christ's love which surpasses knowledge, that you may be filled with all the fullness of God."

Ephesians 3:17-19

V24 Overflow

"The threshing floors will be full of wheat, and the vats will overflow with new wine and oil."

The blessing of the Lord brings abundance. The outpouring of His mercy brings life and peace to us. All our provisions overflow with the goodness of God. From the bread that we eat to the wine that we drink. God has promised that His people will never be without the necessities of life, and He will provide for them.

"I have been young, and now am old, yet I have not seen the righteous forsaken, nor his children begging for bread."

Psalm 37:25

God will also provide for our spiritual desires, which we have now as faithful people of God. God does not just bless His people but pours down His righteousness until there is overflow. The bread of the Word is poured out in abundance and the effect is monumental blessing on the people of God, bringing in those who are being saved. The new wine and the oil of salvation is in full supply – it is the days of renewal and revival. Many long for these days and in our day, they seem so far away. But the Lord is not slow concerning His promise that He will pour out a blessing when we come to Him.

"Bring the whole tithe into the storehouse, that there may be food in my house, and test me now in this," says the Lord of hosts, "if I will not open you the windows of heaven, and pour you out a blessing, that there shall not be room enough for."

Malachi 3:10

We must keep to the Word of God and obey His holy commands. We must bring all our vows to full fruition and keep the commandments of the Lord. Surely, He will encourage us as we come. God is not weary-minded, concerning His promises but give us the encouragements we need to follow what He wants us to do.

The question for us is do we want His blessing? Do we believe it is worth having? Have we become so worldly minded that we cannot conceive of how wonderful it would be?

Beloved, we must call out for the overflow. We must desire it above all else. When we put away our sin and pray to the Lord of the harvest, He will pour out such a blessing we will not be able to contain it, or ourselves.

Lord, come and fill us with your Holy Spirit that we will desire you and only you. May you be our blessing. May your Spirit overflow...

V25 Restore

"I will restore to you the years that the swarming locust has eaten, the great locust, the grasshopper, and the caterpillar, my great army, which I sent among you."

Here we have the incredible. The holy God is so willing and able to bless He can cover over and give back to us the effects of the years of wandering and sin. This is another amazing promise of the Lord. All those years of sinful desire and hurtful behaviour will be covered over by new and glorious memories that blot out the sin and degradation of those days, not to be remembered any more. We have this in this life but to the full extent in the coming kingdom when no hurtful thing will follow the child of God into the full realisation of the coming kingdom.

"They will not hurt nor destroy in all my holy mountain; for the earth will be full of the knowledge of the Lord, as the waters cover the sea."

Isaiah 11:9

In that great day, the mercy of the Lord will be seen and known by all His redeemed people. The years of the devouring of the locust will be over and their destructive influences will be healed. The Lord permitted them to take hold and oppress His people for a specific purpose, to teach them and constrain them to return to their first love of Him.

In our lives also we seek the blessing of the Lord as we turn from our sin and failure and return to fellowship with the Lord. Though our days have been oppressive, and the enemy has pressed in, we overcome by His mighty power and God promises to renew our lives and restore the fellowship with Him.

Beloved, we hold fast to our faith in Christ and the fellowship of walking with Him every day. We keep ourselves in the love of God and look to Him to refresh our life with blessing and the forgetfulness of troubles.

V26 Wondrously

"You will have plenty to eat, and be satisfied, and will praise the name of the Lord, your God, who has dealt wondrously with you; and my people will never again be disappointed."

The Lord is so kind to us and knows it is hard for us to praise when we are hungry, thirsty and tired. He provides liberally for our temporal needs. He is our ever loving and glorious Lord and will not treat us harshly or put us through situations that we cannot handle. Some of those situations will be stressful and strenuous but we face them in the power of the Holy Spirit and not in our own strength.

God gives us all things richly to enjoy and we should enjoy the things that He gives us in the course of our lives. There are some men who would restrict enjoyment and keep the people of God in penury to support their own empires and ideas. This is not God's way, and we resist the impulse to succumb to such folly. There are some who will force their nearest and dearest to suffer for someone else's ideas and cause heartache and stress. This is not how God operates.

God says we will have plenty to eat and be satisfied. We will praise His name for the provision and for the enjoyment of it. God deals with us generously and openly and we are so glad to know him and serve Him. He says that no one who follows Him or lives to praise His name will be disappointed.

There are very great blessings to be had and known through repentance and faith, and the enemy of our souls will keep us blind and insensible with his lies and misrepresentations of the Loving God we serve. He presents God as some kind of spoil sport, and we will live all our lives in misery and destitution if we should follow Him. There are some who live like this to their detriment and the detriment of their families, but this is not the way of God. We are to rejoice every day. We are to be happy in the Lord our God and experience His love through the moments of our days.

Satan is a liar through and through and we listen to him at our own peril. He must not be allowed to steal your peace and joy in the Lord and to treat yourself in a cruel way. We are to be kind and that includes towards ourselves.

V27 In the midst

"You will know that I am in the midst of Israel, and that I am the Lord, your God, and there is no one else; and my people will never again be disappointed."

God will not allow our souls to be lost or for us to be disappointed in our Christian life. It is easy to be disappointed in other Christians and in our church situations, but the Lord is so faithful to us and will not allow us to be cast down and fall away from the faith. We keep our trust in Him and our eyes fixed on our Saviour Jesus. There are many disappointing things that happen, but if our gaze is fixed on what the Lord is doing and in His person we will not be disappointed. Our hope is not in humans but in the Lord Jesus.

We can become disillusioned with the Christian culture and the social situation, and we must not allow that to makes us disillusioned with our life in Christ. We guard our hearts jealously and keep the light of our faith burning brightly in the middle of all turmoil and trials.

As Christian people we are more than bodies but have souls that are now made alive to God, and they must be fed and kept right in fellowship with the Lord. If we are disobedient and disrespectful of the Lord and His ways, we cannot expect to be in that close place of fellowship with Him. This is why it is so important to keep short accounts with the Lord and to be very careful to honour and obey Him who loves us and who we also love in return.

The Lord will be in the very centre of our lives and dwell amongst us with great power and glory. We will be able to see it and our faith will be rampant against the disappointments of life, in that we will not be disappointed in the Lord and His spiritual provision for us. He himself will dwell in the midst of us, in our life, psyche and circumstances. We can trust in him because of who He is and what He has done.

"I heard a loud voice out of heaven saying, "Behold, God's dwelling is with people, and he will dwell with them, and they will be his people, and God himself will be with them as their God."

Revelation 21:3

V28 Pour out

"It will happen afterward, that I will pour out my Spirit on all flesh; and your sons and your daughters will prophesy. Your old men will dream dreams. Your young men will see visions."

There are many in these days who love this verse and consider it to be applicable to the days in which we now live. We are at the end of the gospel era, and the Lord will return soon. God is going to pour out His Holy Spirit in the last days, in a special way that gives access into His mind and heart like no other. There are many who claim this place but are patently false. There are many who want this place but are not willing to fulfil the criteria to possess it.

To be in tune with God requires holiness of life and a heart that is like the heart of God. The carping of our human desires has no hold on us and we live obedient lives unto the Lord. Many grasp out for the name of "prophet" or "priest" but have no intention of practicing obedience or self-sacrifice. They use godless human means to feather their spiritual nest, set themselves up as women or men of God and dupe many into supporting them. We are all too gullible and forget the pictures we have been given in the Scripture of the *"man of God."* They were upheld only by the grace of God and His power. They did not seek their own good but gave up all rights to comfort and acclaim in this sinful world. They were hated and hunted and put to death for their message and demeanour, but God highly exalted them. Do we really want this? Am I prepared for that level of sacrifice and sanctification?

There are some who live like this, but they are not recognised nor acclaimed, but live for God in silence and ignominy. They do mighty deeds but hidden from the glare of public scrutiny and the stultifying effects of celebrity. God has His women and men in every place, and He is raising them to serve Him as He sees fit. He will empower them and give the strength they need and the required faith to serve Him. In these last days we need women and men who will sacrifice the right to recognition in this present evil age and devote themselves to the Word of God and prayer. There are few who want this kind of acclaim from the Lord, but He will personally bless us if we give our lives to Him. We do not seek the publicity of the labels but walk in humility and grace with God.

"But know this, that in the last days, grievous times will come. For men will be lovers of self, lovers of money, boastful, arrogant, blasphemers, disobedient to parents, unthankful, unholy... holding a form of godliness, but having denied its power."

2 Timothy 3:1-2,5

V29 In those days

"And also on the servants and on the handmaids in those days, I will pour out my Spirit."

In these last days of human history, God will pour out His Spirit in a full and free provision. There will be no discrimination between, master and servant, man or woman. The power of the Holy Spirit and the gifting of the Lord does not depend on us or on our education, experiences or status in this life. God is no respecter of persons and will bless those who He chooses, as He also saves to eternal life those people He has set His heart upon.

The pouring out of the Spirit will mean the greater gifts will be in abundance and the fruit of the Spirit will be powerful in the lives of the people of God. There will be people with clarity about the Word of God and powerful prayerfulness. There will be deep understanding of the Truth of God and the powerful and fruitful preaching of the gospel. There will be the raising up of women and men, old and young – all who the Spirit of God should set His heart upon. They will be given the understanding and power of the Spirit to minister in the realm God requires of them, not in the limelight, but quietly and privately in the lives of those around them, who God deigns to listen.

We have had these days of abundance, and now seem to be entering a time of spiritual destitution and lack of the fruit of the Spirit. We could be on the brink of the time of tribulation when the people of God will suffer persecutions and great hardship. The promise of the Word of God is that we will be kept by His power and provided for. The Lord Jesus is coming soon, and we must be ready and glad for His appearing. Only those who are truly the Lord's people will persevere to the end in these powerfully evil days of persecution and oppression of Christian people.

We listen to those who love the Lord and display the fruit of the Spirit in their lives. We support each other, check each other and help each other along the heavenly pathway to reach home with joy and victory. This is the aim of the church of Christ – to bring the elect people into the fellowship and keep ourselves in the love of God.

The gospel age may be coming to a close, so we work doubly hard to bring in the remnant of the people of God and preach the gospel with clarity and persuasiveness. The trumpet must yet sound, for the Lord tarries. There is work yet to be done and souls still to be saved.

Beloved, we cannot tell how our ministry of the Lord will work out so we sow the seed at every opportunity that the gospel will succeed, and the Word of God will not return void.

"In the morning sow your seed, and in the evening don't withhold your hand; for you don't know which will prosper, whether this or that, or whether they both will be equally good."

Ecclesiastes 11:6

V30 Wonders

"I will show wonders in the heavens and in the earth: blood, fire, and pillars of smoke."

There will be physical indicators in the end times that the coming of the Lord is very near. The natural world will become uneasy as if in expectation of its deliverance from the grip of human sin. The New Testament also speaks to us of these phenomena. Matthew, Mark, Luke and the book of Acts tells us about the time after the tribulation when these signs will take place. Peter refers to the prophet Joel in his preaching and Jesus speaks of these events in His teaching also.

"But immediately after the oppression of those days, the sun will be darkened, the moon will not give its light, the stars will fall from the sky, and the powers of the heavens will be shaken; and then the sign of the Son of Man will appear in the sky."

Matthew 24:29-30

The end will come quickly, but the signs will all be there to warn the inhabitants of earth that the Lord is coming imminently.

Beloved, we must all be ready for this time and for the Saviour who will return and be the judge of all the earth.

The book of Revelation tells us that though the signs of His coming are blatant, most will turn away, such is the unbelief that resides in the human heart and the folly that ruins our psyche. Do not wait until your heart is too hard to turn and humble yourself before the Lord but come when He is calling you. Perhaps you hear him now...

Now is the time to repent and be saved, for His Spirit will not always speak to you. Do not delay any longer but repent from your sinful heart and ways and find the freedom that is only found in Christ. He alone is able to save, for He has given His life as a random to set you free.

V31 Day of the Lord

"The sun will be turned into darkness, and the moon into blood, before the great and terrible day of the Lord comes."

These signs will appear just before the end. It is not wise to delay salvation to our perceived last moment. The signs will be very frightening, and everyone will know the end is in sight and Christ will appear to take His Christians away out of the troubles and judgment. But there will also be a time of great hardness of heart and strong delusion in those dreadful days. People will experience great fear, yet their rebellious hearts will still not bend or bow to the Saviour God has sent to us in great love. People will still reject the Lord because of the delusion that abounds and the exclusivity of the mark of the Beast, which will preclude the wearer from entering the kingdom.

Do not wait for the last signs. Jesus calls to us now and now is the day of salvation.

"But he answered them, "An evil and adulterous generation seeks after a sign, but no sign will be given it but the sign of Jonah the prophet. For as Jonah was three

*days and three nights in the belly of the
whale, so will the Son of Man be three
days and three nights in the heart of the
earth."*

Matthew 12:39-40

The final sign of salvation has already
happened – the death and resurrection of
our Saviour, the Lord Jesus. There is no
more signs! People always want more or
some sort of personal sign, but it is evil to
require more than God has provided.
Should you see the sun darkened, it will
only generate fear, as the recent historical
events engender fear, but there will be no
repentance and no more day of salvation.
The Lord will return with a shout and the
trumpet will sound, the last trumpet. The
dead will be raised incorruptible, and the
kingdom will come in all its eternal glory.

Beloved, do not be caught out, or caught
hardened by the deceitfulness of sin.
There is no time to procrastinate. The Lord
still waits, but the hour is almost midnight,
when the cry will go up...

*"Behold, the Lord comes with ten
thousands of his holy ones..."*

Jude 1:14

V32 Whoever

"It will happen that whoever will call on the name of the Lord shall be saved; for in Mount Zion and in Jerusalem there will be those who escape, as the Lord has said, and among the remnant, those whom God calls."

Here is a verse of great certainty. Here is a verse of promise and sure hope. Those who call on the Lord, shall be saved.

"All those who the Father gives me will come to me. Him who comes to me I will in no way cast out."

John 6:37

The promise is secure. Whoever comes to the Lord or salvation will not be turned away. In that holy city of Mount Zion and Jerusalem, there will be the multitude of people who have been delivered from the clutches of sin and have escaped the day of God's fierce wrath. The Lord has promised it, so it is true and will happen. There will be a remnant that will be saved for the coming kingdom, a people of God saved for the Lord Jesus Christ and who will not just escape but entering their rest forever. All judgment will be past for them, and they will enter the inheritance stored up for them in heaven. There they will reign with Christ forever in peace and glory.

Why would we pass up on this? The choice could not be more stark and obvious. Eternal bliss or eternal loss. The offer of mercy goes out to all. Whoever will come and repent and leave their sin, put their trust in the living Saviour will be in that blessed remnant. Not everyone will be saved, only those who will humble themselves and respond to the call of God.

Beloved, the offer could not be clearer.

"Whoever calls on the name of the Lord shall be saved.."

Romans 10:13

It is a certainty and God patiently waits to hear the call of repentant sinners who will seek Him. Do not delay. The days are becoming short, and the messages are not clear. The Word of the Lord calls out to you... escape while there is still time...

Joel Chapter Three

21 verses

Joel Chapter Three

V1 Fortunes

"For, behold, in those days, and in that time, when I restore the fortunes of Judah and Jerusalem,"

In the time of Joel, the Lord was going to restore the fortunes of His people after the judgment and attendant repentance. For us that day is yet to come but we wait for it with patience.

In the full series of events of this frightening end time, the Lord is going to restore the kingdom to his elect people. Gone will be the oppression, side-lining, put downs and bullying. God will turn all things right and His people will be delivered from this present evil age. The days of *"turning the other cheek"* will be over, for all oppression will have ceased. Gone will be the turmoil inside as we fight the sinful urges of self and seek vindication. Enemies will be dealt with, and the sinless and holy kingdom will have come.

The days of liberty and freedom for the people of God will be the overarching spirit of the age. The fruit of the Spirit will reveal itself in every believer and all sin will be finally and forever put away. Our souls and minds will no longer have to wrestle with temptation and weakness, but we will be completely free of it, for the Day of the Lord has come and released all goodness from the dark chains of this world.

This is the future for the people of God in the coming time, when the end of all things is revealed.

V2 The Valley of Jehoshaphat

"I will gather all nations, and will bring them down into the valley of Jehoshaphat; and I will execute judgment on them there for my people, and for my heritage, Israel, whom they have scattered among the nations. They have divided my land,"

The end game for the rebels against the holy God will be played out at the end of all history. The people of God will be vindicated, but the enemies of Christ will be destroyed by Him. There will be the spectre of a dark dawn that will slide swiftly over the landscape and destroy all in its path. The day of the Lord will come as a day of reckoning to those who refuse His overtures of mercy. It could not be a more gloomy outlook and prospect and our ministry of warning must not be silent.

It is described as a day of darkness, gloominess, clouds and thick darkness as the forces of evil muster their last push against the almighty. Such is the blindness of futility and the folly of those who reject God. This last great army will be like no other in number and sheer force of human and demonic power. They will meet for the battle of Armageddon in the valley of Jehoshaphat, like the mighty troops of the billions of locusts that have militated against Israel in the prophet Joel's time. They will gather but not a blow will be struck, for Christ will return with His hosts and put a final end to all aggravation and rebellion against God. There has never been a day like this in human history, nor will there be another one in any of the generations.

Just like this threat of the locusts and the desperation that they wreck on the land, it will go down in history as the greatest battle, but it will also be a non-event.

"The beast was taken, and with him the false prophet who worked the signs in his sight, with which he deceived those who had received the mark of the beast and those who worshiped his image. These two were thrown alive into the lake of fire that burns with sulphur. The rest were killed with the sword of him who sat on the horse, the sword which came forth out of his mouth. All the birds were filled with their flesh."

Revelation 19:20-21

The Lord Himself will wreak havoc and death on those who are His enemies and there will be a retribution never seen before. The door of mercy will be forever shut and there will be no more opportunity to repent. The saints of God will not be involved in the conflict for the battle is the Lord's and He will overcome all His enemies in his own power.

"The horse is prepared for the day of battle; but victory is with the LORD."

Proverbs 21:31

V3 That they may drink

"… and have cast lots for my people, and have given a boy for a prostitute, and sold a girl for wine, that they may drink."

The land that belongs to the Lord has been taken over by the enemy and those who oppose the Lord have grasped the land for themselves. Those who do not believe have taken the people of God into captivity and have stolen away the things that do not belong to them, and now the reckoning has come. The people of God are being used to enable the outsiders to God to have what they desire, and their very lives are being gambled for.

The people of this world will use anything to get what satisfies their desires, and the personal and temporal blessings that they crave. Society will use anything to get what is required or keep people happy no matter who it hurts. God is blamed for the troubles of the world and therefore His people are regarded as to blame as well as the Almighty. The hearts of the people are hardened against the Lord, but He will come in deliverance and sweep it all away soon.

Those who have no regard for God also have no regard for human life. They have taken the weakest and the lowest members of society and have used them for their own ends, making them forced labour and slaves to prostitution and degradation. The most vulnerable are sold for just a pittance and counted as the lowest trading item in their godless marketplaces.

They have done this literally and also spiritually to the people of God, treating them like slaves and oppressing them, and forcing them to live low lives and be brought into a society where they are constantly taken advantage of. Oppression breeds a certain mindset that makes people low and keeps them low. It is the strategy of slavery and the means to keep people in subjection and obedient to their masters. It is melted out on the people of God, but only for a short time.

This is the situation of the church of Jesus, where the Christians are so oppressed by what is going on around them, that they can only look to the Lord for deliverance. We do not take vengeance and we guard our minds and words, even in private, and trust in the Lord's provision for us. We look to him, cry out to Him, for He alone is able to strengthen us and help us to overcome the oppression and the attendant attitudes.

V4 Repayment

"Yes, and what are you to me, Tyre, and Sidon, and all the regions of Philistia? Will you repay me? And if you repay me, I will swiftly and speedily return your repayment on your own head."

God scoffs at the evil-doers who think He does not see and does not care about the justice in any situation. God lingers and gives time to repent, and we think He is neglectful concerning His promises to do right. Tyre and Sidon were rich trading ports, but they are as nothing to the Lord, indeed the whole of the nations are like a drop in a bucket. He is not impressed with the regions of the Philistines, and they can never repay the price of their sin anyway, no matter how much they seek to give back to God what is His.

The nations surrounding His people have turned against them, and therefore turned against the Lord. He asks them how they will repay God for His divine judgment and how they will seek recompense for their ill will towards His people Israel, who are here indicative of his spiritual people.

We find ourselves in this situation, where we are in debt to the Lord and can never repay. It is easy to find ourselves in the wrong attitude towards the Lord and to find ourselves against His people and seeking our own comfort and blessing.

God is not interested in our effort to pay, but only on the fact that we are repentant and seeking to be forgiven by Him. Only He can pay the debt we owe and bring us back to God. God is the author of all salvation and we come to Him in faith to receive forgiveness and spiritual life. This is the only recompense He seeks from us, and the only way we can be forgiven. There is no repayment we can give to Him, but our sin and failure and to allow God to change us and make us as we should be.

V5 Finest treasures

"Because you have taken my silver and my gold, and have carried my finest treasures into your temples,"

There are many instances in the Scripture text where the gold and silver that belongs to God, finds its way into pagan places with pagan nations. Sometimes it is captured by the enemy and taken away and at times the ruler of the nation of God gives it away as collateral for freedom and to reduce the prospect of invasion.

God is not regarded when His sacred items from the tabernacle and temple are taken by the unbelievers. They are desecrated and held in regard as trophies over the people of God and as the means of bringing God down into disrepute. Such as in the case with the King of Babylon, King Belshazzar, who took the sacred objects from the temple of God and used them for His own aggrandisement. He was spoken to by God through the handwriting on the wall, which warned him that his life was forfeit that night.

There are many today who bring the blessed truths of God into disrepute by living unloving and unloved lives. They do not know the grace of God in this life and therefore do not value the deep truths of God and the joy of knowing Him. In these days of darkness and lack of love we need to once again rediscover the peace that passes all understanding and find again the forgiveness that is in Christ alone. There is no other treasure like that treasure and no other valuable *"silver or gold"* like that. We must seek the Lord and keep seeking until He should open the door for us and bring us into His banqueting house once more. There we will find all the treasures of love that do not exist in our modern world. There we will find our God and Saviour to be all that He is and we will enter into the experience of the finest of treasures. We will find the Lord Jesus and be satisfied.

V6 Remove them

"...and have sold the children of Judah and the children of Jerusalem to the sons of the Greeks, that you may remove them far from their border."

The people of God have experienced ethnic cleansing and the strategy of sending them as far away as possible from their homeland so that returning was almost impossible. The children of the nation and the children of Jerusalem have been sold far away into slavery to the gentile nations who live so far away from their home that they cannot find their way back and therefore the land can be taken over by the invading forces.

We are all being sold into slavery by the culture in which we live and the enemy who stalks our footsteps. We are captive to the devil at his will did we but know it. We think we are deciding things about our lives and thinking we are exercising freewill and choosing the kind of lives we like, but we are easily duped.

The enemy has sold us down the river into enemy territory and we are stuck here thinking it is our destiny and that is all there is to it. It is not. We need to realise what is going on and stop being drawn into the sinful mindset of this present evil age and break free from the pressures that corrode our thinking processes and ability to choose freely. Only in Christ are we free to exercise choice and be a people of liberty. No one else can grant us that blessing. It is a curious position to be made free from the slavery on sin by becoming a slave to righteousness. We all serve someone, either the freedom of a holy God or the destitution of the slavery to evil.

Beloved, let is open our eyes and see the enemy within and without and shrug him away from us and embrace the truths of God and the holiness that he requires of us.

V7 Stir them up

"Behold, I will stir them up out of the place where you have sold them, and will return your repayment on your own head;"

No matter how far into destitution we have been sold, our God is able to rescue us. No situation is too desperate or problem unsolvable for Him to bring back and renew. The plans of oppressive people and the enemy that dwells in our own psyche is not too strong for His strength to put down and even make us new again. God can release us from the chains that hold us fast and give us liberty and peace. There are some who live in a prison for a long time and suffer under the heal of oppression and bigotry, but it cannot last for the people of God.

No matter how strong the bonds of the particular oppressor we are strapped to, Christ has overcome all sin and suffering through the sacrifice of Himself on the cross. He has paid the price for the sin of His people therefore they are free.

However, we need the impetus to get us out of the rut we often find ourselves in.

The sense of injustice can do it, although often we are so bowed down, we cannot see over the edge to walk to freedom. Sometimes there will be a strong sense in us of anger at our predicament that it will drive us to get up and do something about it!! Gods will give the motivation and power we need to break free of the bonds and walk back into our lives the better for it all. Those who oppress others will find their repayment coming back on themselves with the recompense that they surely deserve. Gods will protect and vindicate His people and lift them up in His own way at the time He so desires.

V8 Faraway

"... and I will sell your sons and your daughters into the hands of the children of Judah, and they will sell them to the men of Sheba, to a faraway nation, for the Lord has spoken it."

Those who have enslaved the people of God will now find themselves the brunt of the same treatment. God will recompense His people and vindicate their position before Him. Gods will not allow the oppression to run on forever but is working out His eternal purposes for his people. Often His will seems to melt in with the shadows of life and we cannot discern what His purposes are. This is where faith takes hold and walks on even when the future is so dimly lit, we cannot see in front of us. The promises of God forever remain, and we take hold of them as the sure and certain landmarks along the pathway to heaven.

Enemies will never gain the upper hand, even when we are tempted to see it that way. We remain steadfast in the Lord our God and in the many lessons we learn from this Scripture. This lesson is for our encouragement and to help us see the long-term view that God sees. The greater our faith the longer we will see and not be disappointed at the current outworking of circumstances. The Lord is gracious and will bear us up in His strong arms so that we do not succumb to fear and fall into sinful responses to our situations.

When we do fall, He will help us to find the way out and be victorious in His strength thereby building faith, hope and love in God. The enemy will find itself far away, but the people of God will be brought into His tender care.

V9 Prepare for war

"Proclaim this among the nations:
"Prepare for war! Stir up the mighty men.
Let all the warriors draw near. Let them
come up."

The Lord calls for war. He goads the
enemy into the preparation for conflict,
knowing that the outcome is set. He
declares that the mighty men of war
should prepare themselves for the conflict
to end all conflicts, for it is with the mighty
God. He calls all the warriors to get tooled
up for the struggle ahead with Him and to
draw near to the conflict. The Day of the
Lord has finally and irrevocably arrived,
and God is calling the men and women of
war out to the site of the fighting.

The enemy can summon up all the
warriors it can find and all the generals
and soldiers in the armies of the nations,
but they will not put to flight the people of
God. God is telling us this to encourage
us, that He will not allow His people to be
destroyed and finally defeated. The Lord
Himself will fight for them and overcome
all the greatest of warriors that find
themselves in that Valley of Jehoshaphat
and facing the last battle of humankind

against the Lord of the Universe. They cannot succeed, but they still try, for their hearts are hard and full of folly.

The cry goes up. Who will answer it?

All those who oppress the people of God and have no understanding of who God is and of His mighty power. This is the end play...

"I saw an angel standing in the sun. He cried with a loud voice, saying to all the birds that fly in the sky, "Come! Be gathered together to the great supper of God, that you may eat the flesh of kings, the flesh of captains, the flesh of mighty men, and the flesh of horses and of those who sit on them, and the flesh of all men, both free and slave, and small and great."

I saw the beast, and the kings of the earth, and their armies, gathered together to make war against him who sat on the horse, and against his army."

Revelation 19:17-19

V10 "I am strong"

"Beat your plowshares into swords, and your pruning hooks into spears. Let the weak say, 'I am strong.'"

Let the armies of the wicked fool themselves that they stand the slightest chance against the Lord! They are deluded and their wicked hearts have no understanding, nor will they ever have the insight from the Lord to be wise. This is the state of the collective human psyche at the end time. People in myriads who believe in themselves and their own futile thought processes and reject the living God.

"... And for this cause God shall send them strong delusion, that they should believe a lie:"

2 Thessalonians 2:11

The unbelieving people of the world will be led into the last battle by the forces of evil at their own choice, but it is a wretched choice. They have no spiritual light and no insight into the deep things of God and are therefore deluded. The day of peace has passed and now the whole human endgame is facing the war of all wars.

The peaceable words of the Lord are now over. The day of salvation has ended and the door of eternal life for whoever seeks it, is forever shut. In the day of mercy, the command is for peace and reconciliation to God. God calls us to lay down our weapons and come to Him, as is written by the prophet Isaiah.

"He will judge between the nations, and will decide concerning many peoples; and they shall beat their swords into plowshares, and their spears into pruning hooks. Nation shall not lift up sword against nation, neither shall they learn war any more."

Isaiah 2:4

The situation is now reversed, and the opposite state of play now has ensued. The implements of peace and prosperity are now to be used for war. All is for war, for the end has come...

V11 Gather yourselves

"Hurry and come, all you surrounding nations, and gather yourselves together." Cause your mighty ones to come down there, O Lord"

The people of the pagan and false religion of this world are impelled to gather for this last great onslaught against the Lord and His anointed king.

"I saw coming out of the mouth of the dragon, and out of the mouth of the beast, and out of the mouth of the false prophet, three unclean spirits, something like frogs; for they are spirits of demons, performing signs; which go forth to the kings of the whole inhabited earth, to gather them together for the war of that great day of God, the Almighty. "Behold, I come like a thief. Blessed is he who watches, and keeps his clothes, so that he doesn't walk naked, and they see his shame." He gathered them together into the place which is called in Hebrew, Megiddo."

Revelation 16:13-16

The Lord will call the pagan nations to the great valley where they will gather to make their last stand against the Almighty God. They can never succeed, but are gathered there, under the compulsion of the will of God. We must be ready for that day and have our souls ready for the end of all things. All will face this day, but only the redeemed people of God will be kept safe from the following carnage that will envelope the aggressing nations.

The people of God will be kept safe from the aggression because the armies of heaven will come down and fight for them, indeed the Lord Himself will destroy them with a word from His mouth.

"The armies which are in heaven followed him on white horses, clothed in white, pure, fine linen. Out of his mouth proceeds a sharp, double-edged sword, that with it he should strike the nations. He will rule them with an iron rod. He treads the winepress of the fierceness of the wrath of God, the Almighty. He has on his garment and on his thigh a name written, "KING OF KINGS, AND LORD OF LORDS."

Revelation 19:14-16

This will be the most fearful day. But not for the people of God. This is their deliverance day from the oppressions of the wicked. All that has vaunted itself against the Lord will now come to grief and the final end of the matter. God will destroy all who refuse to bend their knees to the Lord Jesus, and they will face the judgement and the last great assize of the wicked.

V12 I sit to judge

"Let the nations arouse themselves, and come up to the valley of Jehoshaphat; for there will I sit to judge all the surrounding nations."

The beast of the sea and the beast of the land is awakening, and the Antichrist is gathering his troops, the nations of the whole world against the cause and person of Christ. God is directing all the proceedings and empowering the nations to have the motivation against the Lord Jesus. They have hardened their hearts against the Lord and now they find they cannot go back, because God has irrevocably hardened them. They are compelled to go to that Valley of Jehoshaphat to face the wrath of the Lord and the ignominy of total rout.

This will be the demonstration of the final outcome of the rejection of the nations of the world of the Lord Jesus Christ. The folly of the human way will be seen to be what it is and will find they can do nothing but bow their knees in force to the Lord of the Universe. The Lord Jesus will have ceased to be the Saviour of the world and will now be its judge. The sentence will be passed. It will be immediate and thorough, for all flesh will die and the carrion birds will pick the flesh off the bodies.

There will be no fighting for the saints of God, for Christ will despatch the sentence from His own mouth and His word will not fail.

"Therefore, son of man, prophesy, and tell Gog, Thus says the Lord God: In that day when my people Israel dwells securely, shall you not know it? You shall come from your place out of the uttermost parts of the north, you, and many peoples with you, all of them riding on horses, a great company and a mighty army; and you shall come up against my people Israel, as a cloud to cover the land: it shall happen in the latter days, that I will bring you against my land, that the nations may know me, when I shall be sanctified in you, Gog, before their eyes."

Ezekiel 38:14-16

God will bring up the forces of evil against His holy people and they will fail. They may come as a mighty army with great intimidation and seeming force, but it will not succeed. The prophet Ezekiel has prophesied this end for the people of earth – all who hate God and refuse Him. God will gain all the glory and honour at this great event and his purposes will finally be seen and known. The LORD will be sanctified before all the human race, and all will know that He alone is the Lord.

"At the time of the end shall the king of the south contend with him; and the king of the north shall come against him like a whirlwind, with chariots, and with horsemen, and with many ships; and he shall enter into the countries, and shall overflow and pass through... But news out of the east and out of the north shall trouble him; and he shall go forth with great fury to destroy and utterly to sweep away many. He shall plant the tents of his palace between the sea and the glorious holy mountain; yet he shall come to his end, and none shall help him."

Daniel 11:40,44-45

At this point there is no hope for the wicked. But we have not reached this point as yet. There is still a door of mercy in Christ that is open to all who repent and believe. The offer of mercy still stands, who would pass it over?

V13+14 Valley of Decision

"Put in the sickle; for the harvest is ripe. Come, tread, for the winepress is full, the vats overflow, for their wickedness is great." Multitudes, multitudes in the valley of decision! For the day of the LORD is near, in the valley of decision."

The scenario is sickening. The bloodletting is sure. The judgment has come in the form of the Lamb of God who has taken away the sin of His people and now calls the wicked out to battle.

"I looked, and saw a white cloud, and on the cloud one sitting like a son of man, having on his head a golden crown, and in his hand a sharp sickle. Another angel came out of the temple, crying with a loud voice to him who sat on the cloud, "Send your sickle, and reap; for the hour to reap has come; for the harvest of the earth is ripe!" He who sat on the cloud thrust his sickle on the earth, and the earth was reaped."

Revelation 14:14-16

The angel with the sickle is none other but our God and Saviour Jesus Christ. He has returned to get for Himself the victory over all wickedness and unbelief. All who resist Him are gathered in like the harvest of bloody grapes and thrown into the wine press of the wrath of God. There is no escape. The offer of salvation is over, and the great day of final reckoning has arrived. Only those who are covered by the precious blood of the Lamb slain for them are safe. They shelter under the mighty wings of the grace of God.

"I saw in the night visions, and behold, there came with the clouds of the sky one like a son of man, and he came even to the ancient of days, and they brought him near before him. Dominion was given him, and glory, and a kingdom, that all the peoples, nations, and languages should serve him. His dominion is an everlasting dominion, which will not pass away, and his kingdom one that which will not be destroyed."

Daniel 7:13-14

The all-conquering Lord has returned to claim His kingdom, His people and all the power and glory. The holiness of God has now overcome all evil and evil is being dealt with in the place of the wrath of God

– the plains of Armageddon. The Lord
Jesus is finally calling out His enemies and
His people are with Him, rejoicing in the
triumph of the name of Christ their all-
conquering Lord and God. He alone is able
to pronounce and execute judgment on
the nations that forget God and He alone
treads the wine press of the punishment
for sin. All will succumb.

*"Why do the nations rage, and the peoples
plot a vain thing? The kings of the earth
take a stand, and the rulers take counsel
together, against the LORD, and against
his Anointed, saying, "Let's break their
bonds apart, and cast their cords from
us."*
*He who sits in the heavens will laugh, The
Lord will have them in derision. Then he
will speak to them in his anger, and terrify
them in his wrath: "Yet I have set my King
on my holy hill of Zion."*

Psalm 2:1-6

The rebellion in every human heart will be
broken and each will face the
consequences of its folly. Those who have
followed the kings of the earth, will now
receive the just recompense for their
treachery against their Saviour and

rightful Lord. The bonds of sin and death will be broken for the people of God, but for the ungodly, they will receive the second death that they have chosen. The Lord will laugh at them and will put them to eternal flight. No one will escape the justice of God, and all will be terrified. The Lord Jesus Christ will be set on high and have His true position over the kings of the earth and all who follow them.

It is called the Valley of Decision, not because they can decide for God, but because their dreadful fate is finally outworked and applied to their souls. Their souls are lost to God for good- such is the terrible and frightening position of God-haters and all who embrace folly.

V15 withdraw their shining

"The sun and the moon are darkened, and the stars withdraw their shining."

Heaven and the created earth hide their eyes from the bloody scene of mass destruction.

The created order obeys its Lord and Maker and becomes darkened like the hearts of the people who have turned against their Lord and God. The emancipation of creation is at hand. After the long centuries of groaning under the weight and effect of sin, it will finally be free.

"The fourth angel sounded, and one third of the sun was struck, and one third of the moon, and one third of the stars; so that one third of them would be darkened, and the day wouldn't shine for one third of it, and the night in the same way."

Revelation 8:12

The darkness seems to prevail for a short time. The ungodliness of the human has taken hold of the inhabitants of earth and the outworking of justice is about to unfold. The people of God return to the earth with their Lord and ride on white horses, robed in white linen as the sign of the inner righteousness that they now possess. The darkness does not affect them, as all fear is past for them and only joy remains.

There will be those that shine brightly, and their star never goes out. They stand in contrast to the seething mass of suffering humanity and know that the justice they love is finally meted out. Those who shine like the heavens do so with the radiance of the Lord Jesus, who has bought their freedom at such a great price. They have suffered for Him and now stand as bright stars in the temple of the Lord in voluntary glory in His person. They shine with the righteousness that they embraced on earth and the sacrificial joy by which they willingly laid down their lives for their Lord.

"Those who are wise shall shine as the brightness of the firmament; and those who turn many to righteousness as the stars forever and ever."

Daniel 12:3

The lights go out on human history, but are shining brightly, forever, in the kingdom of God. Joy reigns supreme and the light of God brightens the way of the redeemed and never goes out...

V16 Stronghold

"The LORD will roar from Zion, and thunder from Jerusalem; and the heavens and the earth will shake; but the LORD will be a refuge to his people, and a stronghold to the children of Israel."

The Lamb of God is now the all-conquering Lion of Judah. The Lord our God roars from Zion against His enemies. He has stayed his hand through the aeons of human history and now the day of grace is over for humankind. All who have trusted in him are safe and secure, kept by the covenant of grace until this final time. God thunders from the holy city of Jerusalem and the full weight of the law and the penalty for sin that it brings, falls on the unrepentant. The still small voice that calls us to repentance and faith, is now replaced by the thunderings of the holy God against the destruction that has been meted against His creation as the result of human sin and rebellion. No more will the wrath of man militate against His holy commandments but will praise Him in the destruction of the wicked.

The whole created order will shake and tremble at the sound of the mighty God.

There will be no place to hide for the day of God's mercy and grace is over. God will not tolerate the sin of the ungodly forever but will bring every human soul into judgement for its lack of fear of Him and its avoidance of repentance.

But the Lord is the refuge of His people. This is the message of comfort and encouragement to the people of God in this message from Joel and also in the book of Revelation. Both the thunderings of the law and judgment are related to us in these texts, but the clarion call is to courage and strength for the people of God, as the LORD Himself is their stronghold in this supreme day of trouble. God will be the eternal refuge of His people because of who He is and because of His many and precious promises. Not one soul will be left out of the eternal kingdom and the glory of the Lord will be revealed in the lifting up of His holy people who He has rescued from sin and death. This is the destiny of all those who belong to God. It is so high and lifted up, we are not permitted to see into the glories that will be ours, but we rejoice in hope and faith. And yet we do know something of these glories, because we walk with Him in His delightful presence each day and rejoice with increasing joy at the blessings of the LORD.

"... But as it is written, "Things which an eye didn't see, and an ear didn't hear, which didn't enter into the heart of man, these God has prepared for those who love him." But to us, God revealed them through the Spirit. For the Spirit searches all things, yes, the deep things of God."

1 Corinthians 2:9-10

God has revealed His blessings to us in our personal lives and we experience His goodness and love to us every day. He gives insight into all those who love Him, and we understand His ways and His heart. We do not know all that waits for us in the coming kingdom, but we have the precious presence of the Lord Jesus and the indwelling Holy Spirit who ministers to us and teaches us.

Beloved, let us not be cast down about anything but rejoice in all that is kept for us and that will soon be revealed. Our Stronghold will keep us to the very end and lift us victorious in His great might.

V17 I am the Lord

"So you will know that I am the LORD, your God, dwelling in Zion, my holy mountain. Then Jerusalem will be holy, and no strangers will pass through her any more."

The coming kingdom will be a unique and everlasting time, a whole eternity with the Lord and His holy people dwelling together in peace and tranquillity and eternal joy. Sin will be gone, forgotten forever, and will never darken our psyche ever again. We will be sure about our Lord and God, and nothing will ever separate us from Him ever again. All souls will praise the Lord, those in heaven with Him and those in hell away from Him. The wrath of man will surely praise Him. If we have any doubts about the goodness and greatness of the Lord, they will have gone. We will see Him who our souls love, in all His beauty and we will be like Him. All the related problems of sin, like doubt, shame and fretting, will all have passed away, not even to be remembered. We will have our hearts desire to be free of the sin that so easily besets us in our life at the moment and have total and forever freedom.

No outsiders will even be passing through our homeland of heaven, but only the redeemed people of the living God, bought with that precious price of blood by their Saviour Jesus. He will be forever on the throne and lifted up with His people to reign forever. It will be complete peace and tranquillity and all judgments will be righteous and fair and all that brings sorrow and death will have long gone.

We will see the Lord and know Him, as the one on the throne of Zion, the city of God and His situation on the holy mountain as the exalted Lord of all. The Jerusalem of God will be a holy place reserved only for those who belong there and want to dwell in the courts of the Lord forever.

"Surely goodness and loving kindness shall follow me all the days of my life, and I will dwell in the Lord's house forever."

Psalm 23:6

Beloved, may we not be cast down by what we see and hear in this life, but have our view transfixed on that coming reality. The kingdom will come, and we make sure we are ready for it and are living our lives in the power of its eternal glory. This world is not our final home, we pass through, so that one day soon, we will pass into the eternal ages of the kingdom where there will be no more grief.

"He will wipe away every tear from their eyes. Death will be no more; neither will there be mourning, nor crying, nor pain, any more. The first things have passed away."

Revelation 21:4

V18 A fountain come forth

"It will happen in that day, that the mountains will drop down sweet wine, the hills will flow with milk, all the brooks of Judah will flow with waters, and a fountain will come forth from the house of the LORD, and will water the valley of Shittim."

This is what is surely coming. When the old order of the filth of sin and death is finally over, the new kingdom of the Lord will take hold and fully come in all its glory. The land of milk and honey will finally arrive, and the people of God will have made it to the other side of the Jordan river in victory. The very mountains and hills will be covered with the vineyards of heaven and the wine and milk will flow into every redeemed soul. The waters of Judah will flow for cleansing and blessing and refreshment. All will be for the enjoyment of the people of God, both practically and spiritually. The hills will literally flow with the blessing of God and the lives of the saints will exhibit the full graces of the Holy Spirit in their walking with God.

The whole renewed earth will be full of the knowledge of the Lord. The word of the Lord will flow like a fountain and water the valley where the Shittim trees grow. Shittim wood is smooth and strong and was used in making the implements in the tabernacle of the Lord. The refreshing streams of the word of God enervate the growing trees that furnish the place of God. That holy Word will always take centre place in the eternal kingdom as the river of gospel truth that runs forever for the people of God. It is like the growing stream in the vision of Ezekiel.

"He brought me back to the door of the house; and behold, waters issued out from under the threshold of the house eastward; (for the forefront of the house was toward the east;) and the waters came down from under, from the right side of the house, on the south of the altar."

Ezekiel 47:1

The water starts as a trickle and become increasingly deep until it is deep enough to swim in. The Word of God will always be relevant, and we shall understand more deeply the truths that are revealed within it. In the heavenly kingdom we shall know even as we are known and God will be our everlasting portion, for His word will be known by us and deeply understood.

"For now we see in a mirror, dimly, but then face to face. Now I know in part, but then I will know fully, even as I was also fully known."

1 Corinthians 13:12

V19 The children of Judah

"Egypt will be a desolation, and Edom will be a desolate wilderness, for the violence done to the children of Judah, because they have shed innocent blood in their land."

In this verse Egypt and Edom are used as examples of nations or groups of people who have oppressed the people of God and inflicted terrible injuries on them including the death sentence. The voice of the martyrs always cries out to the Lord for recompense and restitution. God will bring justice to them at the appointed time. He will execute vengeance for those who have lost their lives because they belong to Him. God does not bring down justice straight away but waits for guilty people to repent and change their ways. He waits, and so we can imagine that He does not see and does not value His people. It can cause us to think that God is not really involved with those He loves, but He waits in His long- suffering mercy. He is not willing that any should perish...

The voices of the Hebrew slaves in Egypt went up to God for some time before He instructed Pharaoh to let the people leave and go to their own appointed land. The oppression of the ungodly seems to go unchecked, but God will release His chosen people at the appointed time.

"Others were tried by mocking and scourging, yes, moreover by bonds and imprisonment. They were stoned. They were sawn apart. They were tempted. They were slain with the sword. They went around in sheep skins and in goat skins; being destitute, afflicted, ill-treated (of whom the world was not worthy), wandering in deserts, mountains, caves, and the holes of the earth."

Hebrews 11:36-38

God's people suffer in every generation, from all kinds of persecutions and stresses and oppression from the prevailing culture of the day. This is the way the Lord Jesus walked and should not we also find ourselves in this same position? We must walk worthy of Him, whatever the prevailing circumstances might be and stay obedient to the heavenly vision. God has all things in view for us and will keep our souls and our hearts right to the end and bring us safely home. He will avenge

His suffering people and justice will be done.

"Rejoice over her, O heaven, you saints, apostles, and prophets; for God has judged your judgment on her." A mighty angel took up a stone like a great millstone and cast it into the sea, saying, "Thus with violence will Babylon, the great city, be thrown down, and will be found no more at all."

Revelation 18:20-21

The systems and structures that oppress the people of God will be destroyed. All who involve themselves with its great evil and oppose the holy God will find themselves on the receiving end of His wrath. God will not permit the lack of regard for the shedding of innocent blood but will bring all perpetrators under the judgment of his holy law. God's people will be free and will be vindicated before the eyes of the watching world. The voice of the martyrs still calls out for vengeance and the Lord will recompense them for their suffering for His sake.

"When he opened the fifth seal, I saw underneath the altar the souls of those

who had been killed for the Word of God, and for the testimony of the Lamb which they had. They cried with a loud voice, saying, "How long, Master, the holy and true, until you judge and avenge our blood on those who dwell on the earth?" A long white robe was given to each of them. They were told that they should rest yet for a while, until their fellow servants and their brothers, who would also be killed even as they were, should complete their course."

Revelation 6:9-11

V20 Inhabited forever

"But Judah will be inhabited forever, and Jerusalem from generation to generation."

The people who belong to God will not lose out.

We may lose our lives and be completely rejected and side-lined, but God will bring us safely to the heavenly land of Judah where we will dwell safely forever.

The generation of the people of God will forever inhabit the promised land, that place prepared for them by their Saviour and Lord.

"Don't let your heart be troubled. Believe in God. Believe also in me. In my Father's house are many homes. If it weren't so, I would have told you. I am going to prepare a place for you. If I go and prepare a place for you, I will come again, and will receive you to myself; that where I am, you may be there also."
John 14:1-3

The promise stands secure for the people of God, and they will surely enter into their inheritance. They will dwell in Judah in the safety of the protection of the Lord and in the holy city where they belong. It will be lived in forever, as the promised land flowing with milk and honey, and the eternal city of God – Jerusalem the golden. The people who dwell there will be an everlasting people for the glory of God and as a perpetual sign of His mercy and righteousness.

"They shall dwell in the land that I have given to Jacob my servant, in which your fathers lived; and they shall dwell therein, they, and their children, and their children's children, forever: and David my servant shall be their prince for ever."

Ezekiel 37:25

The people who are raised from the dry bones in the vision of Ezekiel will be a people for the Lord and He will give them their place and Christ will reign over them forever, as Lord and God.

V21 For the Lord dwells in Zion

"I will cleanse their blood, that I have not cleansed: for the LORD dwells in Zion."

The people of God will be completely cleaned for their remaining taint and daily fight with sin at that time of the full redemption of their body, mind and soul. All the remaining difficulties with sin and self will pass away and they will be made perfect in the Lord. They are the redeemed people, bought with the precious blood of Christ and now made perfect in the heavenly kingdom. This will be the relief and glory of the saints of God- that their sin is finally and forever purged away, and they are free from the cloying effects on their souls. They will be set free from it. The victory of the cross of Christ will now have its full effects and the souls of His people will be set free.

God will do this because this is the full intent of His purposes in salvation. To bring to pass a holy people, for His name sake and for the glory of the Lord Jesus Christ who died for them. As the Lord dwells in Zion, so will they, in full vigour and in the power of the Holy Spirit of God.

Beloved, the root and cause of sin will finally be dealt with and put away from the psyche of the people of the Lord and they will be holy through and through. This is the destiny of all who love the Lord and His commandments. We will be free and be able to worship the Lord in the beauty of holiness forever. All who love the LORD love this.

"Seek the LORD while he may be found; call you on him while he is near: let the wicked forsake his way, and the unrighteous man his thoughts; and let him return to The LORD and he will have mercy on him; and to our God, for he will abundantly pardon."

Isaiah 55:6-7

Printed in Great Britain
by Amazon